presents

THE SUMMER HOUSE

A Comedy Thriller

Devised by **Will Adamsdale**, **Neil Haigh**,
Matthew Steer and **John Wright**
Performed by **Will Adamsdale**,
Neil Haigh and **Matthew Steer**
Directed by **John Wright**
Designed by **Michael Vale**
Lighting design by **Ian Scott**
Music and sound design by **Chris Branch**
Production Management by **Jeremy Walker**

The Summer House was first performed at artsdepot,
London, on 11th March 2011.

Commissioned by Corn Exchange Newbury. Developed as
part of Fuel at the Roundhouse and the Jerwood Residencies
at Cove Park which are supported by the Jerwood Charitable
Foundation. Funded by Arts Council England. Production
time in kind provided by artsdepot.

Presented as part of the Gate Guests Season 2012

Artist biographies:

Will Adamsdale's first solo show, *Jackson's Way*, won the Perrier Award in 2004. In January 2011 he completed *Jackson's Way: The London Jacksathon!* a 26 day, 26 venue tour of London. His other shows have been *The Receipt*, a collaboration with sonic artist Chris Branch (Fringe First, Brits Off Broadway), and *The Human Computer*. Other theatre credits include *Waters of the Moon* (Salisbury Playhouse), *Faster* (Filter/BAC/Lyric studio/Tour), *Ben Hur* and *The World Cup Final 1966* (BAC), *The Winslow Boy* and *Arcadia* (Chichester Festival Theatre), *Notes from Underground* (Trafalgar Studios). Will's film credits include *The Wild and Wycked World of Brian Jones*, *The Boat That Rocked*, *Four Lions* and *Skeletons*. He recently co-wrote and performed a new drama for Radio 4, *Earls of Court*. He gave directing advice to Stewart Lee on *What Would Judas Do?* and Josie Long on *Be Honourable!*
willadamsdale.com

Neil Haigh trained at Middlesex University and is an actor, director, improviser and writer. TV credits include: *Dalziel & Pascoe* and *Casualty* (BBC), *No Angels* (C4), *The Bill* (ITV) and a year talking to a little version of himself as the face of Abbey in *Me & My Money*. Theatre credits include: *Richard III* (UK Tour) with Third Party & John Wright, *Increased Difficulty of Concentration* (Gate Theatre), Beckett's *Catastrophe* (Gate Theatre), *A Midsummer Night's Dream* (UK Tour), *Rice/Oil Field* (Vesturport/ Paines Plough, Trafalgar Studios), *The Windmill* (Manchester Royal Exchange), *Fair Maid of the West* (Third Party), *Spittoon* with Gavin Robertson, *Stalingrad* (Dead Earnest/Crucible Sheffield). Neil has also devised and acted in *Hard Hearted Hannah* (Lyric Hammersmith/Kennedy Centre Washington DC), *Pub Rock* (Lyric Hammersmith & UK), *Meat & 2 Veg (*BAC, UK Tour, Hong Kong*)*, *Ratcatcher of Hamelin* (BAC) – all with Cartoon de Salvo with whom he is an Associate Artist, and the award-winning solo show *Angels of the Universe* (Gate Theatre, Budapest, Edinburgh) which he adapted from the novel of the same name. He worked with Richard Jones on the development of the Young Vic show *Annie Get Your Gun* and has directed comedian Alun Cochrane as well as theatre shows in Reykjavik, Edinburgh & London for Icelandic Take Away Theatre. Following this run, Neil will be appearing with Cartoon de Salvo in April at Soho Theatre in their improvised storytelling show, *Made Up.*

Matthew Steer has been acting professionally since the age of eleven. He has previously collaborated with John Wright playing Hamlet in *Hamlet* (UK Tour), *Richard III* (UK Tour) and *The Changeling* (BAC), all for Third Party Productions.

Other theatre credits include co-writing and performing in *Britain's Best Mates* (Pleasance, Edinburgh Fringe), *Immortal* (Theatre Museum, Covent Garden), *My Love DMZ* with Korean company Mokhwa (Rose, Kingston), *Out of the Blue* (Liverpool Everyman), *The Steppe Brothers* (Edinburgh Fringe) and *Shades* (Albery).

His TV credits include *EastEnders, Misfits, Silent Witness, The Royal,* *Summerhill, Black Hearts in Battersea, Casualty, The Bill, Doctors,* and the voice of Private Popper in CBBC's BAFTA-nominated *Big Babies.* Matthew also co-wrote and performed in the Comedy Central series *Britain's Best Mates.* Films include *Basil, An Exchange of Fire,* Disney's *Spies* and *Harry Potter 7.*
matthewsteer.com

John Wright is co-director of Beehive, with Toria Banks. Their most recent productions include: *Dr Faustus* (Winner of the Peter Brook Award) and *The Fragility of X* (winner of The Spirit of the Fringe Award). John was co-founder of Trestle Theatre Co. in 1980 and directed most of their work until 1990 when he co-founded Told by an Idiot and directed: *On the Verge; I'm so Big; You Haven't Embraced Me Yet; Don't Laugh it's My Life; Aladdin; Happy Birthday Mr. Decca D; I Can't Wake Up,* and *Papa Mass.* Other productions include: *Common Nonsense* (Reykjavik City); *King Ubu* (Gate); *Out of the Blue* (Rejects Revenge at Liverpool Everyman); *Beauty and the Beast* (Belgrade, Coventry) ; *Skinless (*Oval House); *Meeting Myself Coming Back* (Soho); *The Shoe,* and *Father Christmas and the Last Present* (Polka). Opera includes: *Master Peter's Puppets* and *Aesop* (ROH and National Youth Music Theatre); *Arcane New Opera* (Opera Circus). Publications include *The Voices of the Archetypes* (Oak Leaf Audio Projects); *The Masks of Jacques Lecoq* (Routledge) and *Why is That so Funny?* (Nick Hern). John is currently finishing *Acting Without Bullshit* (Nick Hern). Awards include a Greater London Arts Award for contribution to physical theatre; a Fringe First for *Aesop*; Time Out Theatre Award for *The Edge*; a Guardian and Sunday Times Award for *She'll be Coming Round the Mountain*; and Best New Work Award at Hong Kong International Arts Festival for *Shooting Sons.*

Michael Vale has designed the sets and costumes for over 170 theatre and opera productions both in the UK and abroad including those he has directed. Companies he has worked with include: RSC; NT; ROH; ENO; Glyndebourne Festival Opera; Opera North; Los Angeles Opera; New Zealand International Art's Festival; Galaxy Theatre, Tokyo; Warsaw Globe Theatre Company; Lyric; Almeida; Manchester Royal Exchange; West Yorkshire Playhouse; Sheffield Crucible; Liverpool Playhouse; Nottingham Playhouse; BOV; Plymouth Theatre Royal; Edinburgh Royal Lyceum; Bolton Octagon; Oldham Coliseum; Manchester Library Theatre; Salisbury Playhouse; Colchester Mercury Theatre; The Royal Festival Hall; The Queen Elizabeth Hall; English Touring Theatre; English Touring Opera; BAC; Told By An Idiot, Spymonkey and Kneehigh. His work has been nominated for two Olivier Awards; a Charrington Fringe First Award; an Irish Times Theatre Award and a Manchester Evening News Theatre Award.

Ian Scott has designed the lighting for numerous theatre companies including: Paines Plough; NT; Traverse; Almeida; NYT; Abbey; Nottingham Playhouse; Salisbury Playhouse; Greenwich; David Glass Ensemble; Polka; Unicorn; LIFT; Theatre Royal Plymouth; Gecko; Stan Won't Dance; Northern Stage; Liverpool Everyman; Menier Chocolate Factory; and West Yorkshire Playhouse. An Associate Artist of Suspect Culture, Ian designed both set and lighting for *Timeless; Mainstream* and *Lament.*

Chris Branch is one half of writing duo Brains and Hunch with Tom Haines. Over the last eight years they have composed sound design for film, TV and theatre. Recent film credits include: feature film *Buried Land*, director Steven Eastwood, premiered at the 2010 Tribeca Film Festival and short film *Love Hate*, directors Blake & Dylan Ritson. Commercial credits include: work for the BBC and *IOC – All Together Now*, an animated film for the Olympics 2010. Recent theatre credits include: *Joseph K* (Gate Theatre); Filter Theatre's *Three Sisters* (Lyric Hammersmith); *Julius Caesar* (RSC). **brainsandhunch.com**

Jeremy Walker trained at Central School of Speech and Drama in Designing for the Stage. He works for a range of companies and theatres collaborating in developing new shows. He was involved in the development of Gecko's *The Arab & the Jew* and was production manager on their spring tour. Other production management work includes: *Not for Me, Not for You, But for Us; Big Stories; One On One Festival; N2O; David Lynch Lock In* (BAC); *Ether Frolics* and *Kursk* (Edinburgh 2009) for Sound&Fury; *Under Glass* (Clod Ensemble); *ARC, Memento Mori, Every Action* (Ockham's Razor); *Irish Giant, Pub Rock* and *Made Up* (Cartoon de Salvo); *Cupid 2011* (Subject to Change) and *The Simple Things in Life* (Latitude, Big Chill and Edinburgh 2011) for Fuel.

·⌐fueL

The Summer House is produced by **Fuel**. Fuel produce fresh work for adventurous people by inspiring artists. Founded in 2004 and led by Louise Blackwell and Kate McGrath, Fuel is a producing organisation working in partnership with some of the most exciting theatre artists in the UK to develop, create and present new work for all.

Fuel is currently producing projects with Will Adamsdale, Belarus Free Theatre, Clod Ensemble, Inua Ellams, Fevered Sleep, David Rosenberg, Sound&Fury, Uninvited Guests and Melanie Wilson.

Fuel's recent projects include: *The Simple Things in Life* (various artists); *Minsk 2011: A Reply to Kathy Acker* (Belarus Free Theatre, Edinburgh 2011); *Jackson's Way* (Will Adamsdale); *Electric Hotel* (Requardt & Rosenberg); *Kursk* and *Going Dark* (Sound&Fury); *MUST: The Inside Story* (Peggy Shaw and Clod Ensemble); *Love Letters Straight From Your Heart* (Uninvited Guests); *The Forest* and *On Ageing* (Fevered Sleep); *The 14th Tale* and *Black T-Shirt Collection* (Inua Ellams); *An Anatomie in Four Quarters* (Clod Ensemble) and *Autobiographer* (Melanie Wilson).

In partnership with higher education organisations, Fuel runs a rolling internship scheme. Our current producing intern is Hannah Myers from Central School of Speech and Drama. For further information on Fuel, our artists, our team and our internships, please visit www.fueltheatre.com or call 020 7228 6688.

"One of the most exciting and indispensable producing outfits working in British theatre today."
Guardian

"The maverick producing organisation who are prepared to invest in adventurous artists."
The Herald

Directors **Kate McGrath** & **Louise Blackwell**
Executive Director **Ed Errington**
Producer **Christina Elliot**
Head of Production **Stuart Heyes**
Project Managers **Alice Massey** & **Rosalind Wynn**
Deputy Production Manager **Ian Moore**
Administrator **Natalie Dibsdale**

Make Your Mark on Fuel:

At Fuel we are constantly working with artists to create new experiences for you to enjoy. We believe in these aims and work hard every day to make them happen. If you would like to make your mark, visit our website at fueltheatre.com and click on 'support'. There are lots of ways you can get involved. Just £5 a month will help make our ambitions real. In return we'll give you exclusive benefits and the inside story on what we're up to. You'll make great ideas come to life for the broadest possible audience.

You'll keep us going.

To get involved, please download the Make Your Mark form from the Fuel website: www.fueltheatre.com

Thank you from all of us.

A big thank you to our current supporters

   JERWOOD CHARITABLE FOUNDATION

Fuel receives National Portfolio funding
from Arts Council England

With thanks to our Catalysts:
Sean Egan, James Mackenzie-Blackman,
Michael Morris, Sarah Preece, Sarah Golding,
John Tiffany and Nick Williams.

GATE
THEATRE NOTTING HILL

About The Gate

"Queue, cajole or fight to get into this theatre"
The Sunday Times

The Gate is the UK's only small-scale theatre dedicated to producing a repertoire with a wholly international focus, meaning it occupies a unique position within Britain's diverse theatrical landscape. With an average audience capacity of 70, the Gate continues to challenge and inspire artists, making it famous for being one of London's most flexible and transformable theatre spaces.

For over 30 years, the Gate has been a powerhouse in British theatre, serving as a unique engine-room for talent. From directors at the early stages of their careers to exceptional actors, writers and designers all eager to create innovative and inspiring work, the Gate has always been a home for the spirited and anarchic souls of British theatre.

As the Gate's newest Artistic Director, Christopher Haydon continues the Gate's tradition of creating first-class and original theatre.

Artistic Director: **Christopher Haydon**

Executive Director: **Kate Denby**

Producer: **Rachael Williams**

Community Projects Director: **Emma Higham**

Production Assistant: **Katie MacKinnon**

Finance Assistant: **Adam Lilwall**

Duty Managers: **Roisin Caffrey**, **Susan Keats**,
Katie MacKinnon, **Alasdair Macleod**, **Kate Monro**,
Annabel Williamson

Box Office: **Priya Jethwa**, **Sheena Khanna**, **Charlotte Lund**,
Danielle Lynch, **Eilis Sanfey**

Press: **Kate Morley at Blueprint PR**

FOREWORD

Devising has always been the poor relation of dramatic writing. In fact many people refuse to acknowledge that devising could ever be a literary activity at all. They see it as some kind of fixed improvisation unique to the people doing it at the time as opposed to making something so valued that others might like to do it again in their way. Not all writing is the product of a solitary imagination and a computer. We started with the premise that devising is a process of collaborative writing. *The Summer House* is our attempt to devise a play: a piece of dramatic literature that's transferable and worthy of being recreated again, by another group of people. We wanted the language to be of equal importance as the action and situations to grow as much out of the text as the action.

This idea demanded an entirely different approach. I found myself consciously breaking all the rules and habitual devising processes – there were no warm-ups, no physical improvisations or provocative games to make something happen. Instead we evolved the habit of sitting in a circle, with a cup of coffee, discussing the story which would soon develop into an improvised dialogue, at which point I'd move my chair back until the idea faded away, and then the process would start all over again. Gradually we started to remember the exchanges we found particularly effective. Then we'd try to put the scene on its feet and play it in the space. Jeremy, our Production Manager, would notate everything that was said and done. All our rehearsals tended to follow that pattern and it became a working method that the company adhered to throughout the tour. Each performance was subjected to the same scrutiny and revision.

It sounds a vague and superficial process, and distinctly 'hands off' from the director's point of view. I must admit, it was painfully slow. Our first run-through lasted about three hours. But the term 'group discussions' hides the diligence that kept the work in a perpetual state of development. It has to be said, this is a risky business that would have easily fallen apart with a less skilled and less experienced team. As it was, Neil, Matt and Will have all been generating their own material for years and they all have considerable dramaturgical skills. My job was to facilitate rather than direct. After all, you can't direct something before it's been written without wrecking the collaborative energy that generated the work in the first place. The story evolved in the room from an idea provided by Neil, and a plot that was inspired by *Goldilocks and the Three Bears*.

John Wright

Special thanks to:
Kate McGrath for script advice, Toria Banks
for directing help, Holly 'Dave' McGrane in Bristol,
Gunnar Helgason for the Icelandic, Vicky Adamczyk
and Matt Jameson-Evans.

This is an accurate presentation of our script at the time of going to press. We've included quite detailed stage directions but – if you're mounting a production – feel free to alter these as seems useful.

John, Neil, Matt and Will

THE SUMMER HOUSE

Devised by Will Adamsdale, Neil Haigh,
Matthew Steer and John Wright

THE SUMMER HOUSE

A Comedy Thriller

OBERON BOOKS
LONDON

WWW.OBERONBOOKS.COM

First published in 2012 by Oberon Books Ltd
521 Caledonian Road, London N7 9RH
Tel: +44 (0) 20 7607 3637 / Fax: +44 (0) 20 7607 3629
e-mail: info@oberonbooks.com
www.oberonbooks.com

A catalogue record for this book is available from the British
Library.

ISBN: 978-1-84943-175-0

Cover image by Edmund Collier

Printed and bound by CPI Group (UK) Ltd, Croydon, CR0 4YY.

SECTION 1

CAR SCENE – THE MERITS OF DYLAN

OVERTURE

JOMSVIKING QUEUE 1

ARRIVAL

HOT TUB 1 – MEN

JOMSVIKING QUEUE 2

HOT TUB 2 – STRANGE ART

OUTING OF NEIL

WILL AND MATT ATTEMPT TO TAKE CONTROL

SECTION 2

THE TRAGIC MYTH OF THUNKATAR & YGDRASIL

AN UNCOMFORTABLE TRUTH EMERGES/ NEIL
LEAVES

HOT DOGS/ NORTHERN LIGHTS/ WILL LEAVES

THE WILDERNESS

THE OFFERING

NEIL RETURNS – SACRED LAND

RITUALS

JOMSVIKING QUEUE 3

HOT TUB 3 – SO WHERE'S THE NEXT BATTLE BOYS?

CHAOS SONG

Running time: 90 minutes with no interval

The stage is set, end on to the auditorium, with fitted wooden rostra of three levels and on a slight diagonal angle to the audience. These are used to represent the summer house itself. Furthest downstage there are two rostra together representing the outdoor veranda. Next to these are three customised white plastic outdoor chairs used as seats in the hot tub. Beside the chairs there is a wallpaper steamer, which is microphoned. When switched on this provides both the steam and noise of the hot tub. Immediately behind and slightly higher there are four wooden rostra. This level represents the interior of the house, along with the tallest and thinnest final rostra furthest upstage. On the mid level are three wooden chairs. USC there is a metal stepladder attached to the rostra.

UR of the rostra there is a freestanding black screen behind which are various hidden items revealed through the course of the play including the RAVEN. Attached to the front of this there is a dot matrix screen, which is not in use as the play begins.

DR there is a freestanding miniature model of the house raised on a small table.

Around the rest of the playing space are various visible items used throughout the play, such as a working microwave with two hot dogs placed inside, a rock in a tub of water, a freestanding microphone DSL.

On the veranda, DS, there is a delicately placed plastic Viking helmet, which has lost one of its two horns, and a toy blue car.

When the audience enter the stage is bare and both sets of chairs and the ladder are covered with plastic dust sheets in the pre set lighting state. Pre show music is 'Hurricane' by Bob Dylan and possibly a couple of other tracks from the album, 'Desire'.

Music fades out. The three performers enter in darkness and take the dust sheet off the wooden chairs SC, rearrange the chairs and sit. NEIL and WILL sit on the furthest downstage two, MATT sits on the up stage one. MATT has a box of 6 bottles of beer which rattle & a map he studies.

Concentrated light only on the three. They are in a car. The strains of 'I Wanna Be Adored' by The Stone Roses can be heard from the car stereo, along with the wind. NEIL is driving and they are clearly abroad as he is seated on the 'wrong' side. All three are English, however, though NEIL is from the north.

Throughout the performance, all the recorded sound effects that are not music tracks are made by human voice – i.e. 'shh' sliding door noises, wind effects etc – or are made on stage with live microphones).

CAR SCENE – THE MERITS OF DYLAN

WILL: *(He is now wearing the Viking helmet.)* STAG!!! Where are they?

(MATT shouts random places from the map like 'Hveragerdi' or 'Laugadalur'. His pronunciation is bad but NEIL tries to encourage him with a 'Not bad'.)

WILL: OK, Neil, top three Dylan albums. Go!

NEIL: Ah. Erm. *Blood on the Tracks, Desire, Blonde on Blonde.*

WILL: Interesting...interesting...and you wouldn't think of including one of the early albums... *(Noticing out of the window.)* COW!

(During this exchange MATT distributes a bottle of beer each to WILL and NEIL, then looks out of the window.)

MATT: COW!

WILL: Is that a cow?

MATT: Where?

WILL: *(To NEIL.)* Do they have cows here?

NEIL: Sort of cows.

WILL: Sort of cows?

MATT: *(Head back in the map.)* Vestmuru...? Estmur. Hmm...

NEIL: What are you trying to say Matthew? You can't just make it up.

WILL: I'd be including one of the early albums in my top three...but at the expense of what?

NEIL: Well, exactly.

MATT: Borgafjordur...

WILL: Matthew we have left the city! We are no longer on the map. I'm confiscating this.

(WILL grabs the map and tries to look at it by his open window but the wind snatches it away and it blows off US behind the screen.)

MATT: Oh. Well that's just great!

WILL: *(Rolls up window, noise of the wind quietens but remains.)* It blew out of my hand! SHEEP!

MATT: Sheep!

WILL: Is that a sheep?

MATT: Where?

WILL: Do they have sheep here?

NEIL: They definitely have sheep. OK, I'm going to hang a left somewhere around here.

MATT: *(Leaning towards the front.)* Neil, we had ourselves a convoy.

WILL: We got ourselves a convoy!

MATT: Well, we don't appear to anymore.

(He and WILL look out the back of the car at the empty road behind them.)

NEIL: *(Talking to MATT in his central mirror whilst driving.)* I gave them directions.

WILL: Where are they?

NEIL: Ah, here we go. *(He turns the car left off the main road.)*

NEIL: I can't see a bloody thing.

(Straining to see in the dark and the snow, he hands the beer back to MATT and turns the music down to concentrate. The road is a little bumpier now and they are going more slowly.)

WILL: Yeah I'd probably include the freewheelin' *Bob Dylan*, not so much because it's a better album per say but...

NEIL: Nah. That's not really my thing...wait...hold on, this isn't right.

(They stop suddenly. NEIL gets out and goes to look in the darkness.)

WILL: You see, Matt...

MATT: I don't want to hear about it!

WILL: You don't know what I'm going to talk about!

MATT: It will be Dylan related.

WILL: It is Dylan related.

MATT: Well I'm out.

(NEIL gets back in.)

NEIL: Right… *(Starts reversing.)*…that's why you don't go off road at night in this country…I've just nearly driven us into Kingsjungar Crevice.

(NEIL changes gear and pulls forward again, turning to drive alongside it.)

WILL: Massive great hole!

MATT: Crevice!

WILL: Crevice!!

MATT: That's enormous!

(The two of them watch it recede.)

NEIL: *(Straining to see.)* OK. It should be just down here somewhere.

(Silence. Driving.)

NEIL: Ah. There it is.

(Music stops abruptly. WILL takes a torch out of his pocket and turns it on, illuminating NEIL's hand on a toy blue car placed on the wooden stage near where they are seated. NEIL draws back the car and releases it. The car takes off across the stage and the torch beam follows it in the dark until it stops DSC/DSR. The model summer house is also lit.)

(General lights fade up, along with a waltz which underscores the following and all the Viking scenes. NEIL smiles at the audience. The three of them now address the audience directly; they are slightly shambolic, perhaps a shade unreliable, as storytellers.)

OVERTURE

NEIL: Now, I don't know how much you know about Norse mythology, but one thing that the Vikings believed was that the world was licked into existence by a cow.

(MATT has dissolved the car by arranging the wooden chairs back into a straight line before popping up behind them with a cow mask on and seeming alarmed.)

(Meanwhile, WILL has disappeared upstage and behind the black screen.)

You've probably heard of Odin, the one-eyed god, who would send his pet raven to spy on the world and report back to him.

(A RAVEN appears suddenly in a light above the screen.)

And you've probably heard of Thor. Thor, of course, was the god of war.

(By now MATT has thrown the cow mask behind the screen and wraps the dustsheet on the ladder around him as a cloak. NEIL places the one-horned plastic Viking helmet on MATT's head to complete the look.)

MATT: Ah Loki. How do I look?

NEIL: *(Assuming the role of LOKI, the trickster god.)* It's kind of bunched up too much but it's a good length. You should check Odin's out; he's definitely got something going on.

MATT: *(Petulant.)* Oh, he wears his so bloody well

NEIL: How's your wife by the way?

MATT: *(Highly suspicious.)* She's fine.

NEIL: Oh good.

MATT: *(About to confess.)* Actually…

(The RAVEN appears as before.)

…it's anything but fine.

(LOKI signals and THOR sees the RAVEN.)

…never mind.

(The RAVEN disappears.)

NEIL: Thor was notoriously bad tempered…

(THOR slips on ladder, curses.)

MATT: Where's my bloody hammer!?

NEIL: …and, as he controlled the weather, the weather was pretty bad tempered too.

(WILL behind the screen operates the leaf blower on THOR, making his cape billow wildly and THOR curse more with frustration.)

(WILL appears from behind the screen.)

WILL: Now all that was up in 'Godland', or Asgaard, and the next level down was Valhalla, or the 'Mead Hall of the Slain', where warriors who had died bravely in battle partied away for eternity.

(MATT and WILL stand on the upper rostra – Valhalla – and briefly party.)

MATT: Next down was earth *(Stepping down a level.)* which you might be surprised to hear wasn't just the realm of man but armies of elves, three wise squirrels, and also…

(Pause. WILL steps down too. His footsteps are amplified.)

…Giants.

(More footsteps.)

(WILL as a giant notices the blue toy car and picks it up to inspect it.)

(NEIL steps off the rostra DSL and transforms into a female giantess.)

NEIL: Oh Thunkatar my darling.

(WILL sees his sweetheart and, placing the car back down SR steps off the rostra on the opposite side.)

WILL: Ygdrasil my sweet. Just two weeks till our wedding day.

NEIL: The giant wedding of the century I can hardly wait.

WILL: Oh my sexy giantess.

NEIL: Take me!

WILL: What, now?

NEIL: Yes now, fly over this ocean and take me.

WILL: I'm coming Ygdrasil!

NEIL: No, we must wait.

MATT: But more than anything there were lots and lots of Vikings, not all of them were particularly fierce, some just went about their daily business.

(MATT throws the Viking helmet to WILL.)

NEIL: Oi, spear dodger!

MATT: Are you going to join this next battle or what?

NEIL: You're never going to make it to Valhalla like that.

WILL: *(Distributing fake snow downstage.)* Well somebody has got to feed these chickens.

NEIL: *(To the audience, resuming narrator duty.)* So as you've probably gathered it was a fairly macho society…and we haven't even got to the Jomsvikings yet.

JOMSVIKINGS 1

(WILL and MATT become calm, fearsome Jomsvikings side by side.)

NEIL: The Jomsvikings were the SAS of the Viking world, a close-knit band of brothers, loyal only to each other and whose word was their absolute bond. They were prone to random acts of violence and –

(MATT's bored Jomsviking stabs NEIL in the gut and he dies.)

WILL: One evening the Jomsvikings got so drunk that they decided to invade Norway the next morning. *(To MATT.)* Are we in?

MATT: Yeah! Are we all in?

NEIL: *(Springing back to life, now as a drunken Jomsviking also.)*
Yes!

(They place hands one on top of each other.)

WILL: A promise is a promise.

ALL: A pledge is a pledge.

(MATT mimes driving a knife through all three hands.)

ALL: Aaaaah!

WILL: The next morning…

(As he becomes the narrator and attempts to walk away he pulls the others with him due to the knife still wedged through their hands. He mimes taking the knife out.)

So, the next morning, nursing vile hangovers the Jomsvikings trudged down to the beaches, got into their longboats and rowed to Norway. Because a promise is a promise…

NEIL & MATT: *(Now seated on the middle rostra, rowing unenthusiastically with hangovers.)* And a pledge is a pledge.

WILL: When they arrived they were of course soundly trounced by Norway's numerically vastly superior army and those who survived were led off to their executions in front of the king of Norway.

(The three, hands tied, form a line and defiantly begin to sing/chant as they walk to their deaths.)

MATT: We are going to!

ALL: Valhalla!

MATT: We are going to!

ALL: Valhalla!

MATT: Give me a 'V'!

NEIL & WILL: 'V'!

MATT: Give me an 'A'!

NEIL & WILL: 'A'!

(They all pause and consider the spelling.)

MATT: We are going to!

ALL: Valhalla!

MATT: Hold up, hold up we've got ourselves a queue.

(They bang into each other as they stop suddenly DSL next to the lower rostra.)

WILL & NEIL: What?

MATT: *(Shouting down the imaginary queue.)* Egil, what's the score? *(Pause.)* OK, they are doing us one by one.

WILL: What?

NEIL: They've got one axeman?

MATT: Yep.

WILL: For all of us?

NEIL: That's gonna take bloody ages!

WILL: Norweigans!

MATT: Amateurs.

(General dismay.)

NEIL: *(Talking behind WILL to the others we imagine are also in the line.)* They've got one axe man. Yeah, pass it down, one axe man for the lot of us.

(Pause. WILL sees a Jomsviking he hasn't run into in a while a long way down the queue.)

WILL: Tord! Tord!

NEIL: *(Looking to the front of the queue, off DSR, as the first execution is about to happen.)* Here we go. Who's up?

MATT: *(Looking too.)* It's Olaf.

ALL: *(As a football crowd watching the wind up to a goal kick from the stands.)* Whoooooooooooaaaaah… Oh! *(They interrupt the rhythm suddenly as the beheading is botched appallingly.)*

WILL: Scalped him!

NEIL: Oh, what! No!

MATT: Don't keep hacking at him.

NEIL: Put him out of his misery… *(The beheading is completed.)*

ALL: Thank you/finally/yes.

(The execution over they face out once more.)

NEIL: I've a good mind to get up there and do it myself.

(Sudden gust of wind – sound effect.)

(NEIL and WILL react as though flicked in the face by MATT's long viking locks. MATT continues to heroically face out.)

WILL: Ah, mate your hair!

MATT: What??

WILL: It flicks out in the wind.

MATT: You love it.

WILL: Yes, we do love it, it's famed across the land as a symbol of the tribe.

NEIL: yes, it's long, it's beautiful, it's luxurious, now tie it up or something!

MATT: Oh, shush.

(Pause.)

NEIL: Looks like we're going to be here for a while.

WILL: Tord! Tord!

(Blackout. Viking waltz music snaps out with the lights.)

ARRIVAL

(We are now back with three main characters, who are now inside the summer house. They have just shut the front door behind them and giggle in the darkness.)

(Giggling in the darkness.)

WILL: Neil, you said it was an hour.

NEIL: More or less. Just watch your step.

> *(WILL slips over in the dark with a grunt.)*

MATT: Man down, Neil!

WILL: I am so cold. Do you know how much these hands are worth?

NEIL: Take your shoes off.

MATT: Yes sir, Neil sir.

WILL: Take us to the light and the warmth.

> *(NEIL, DS, picks up the toy car and places it beside the model, in front of the house. It is now clear that this is a miniature version of the house they are in.)*

MATT: I am going in.

WILL: No wait.

NEIL: *(Walking back US and past them both, then disappearing behind the screen.)* I'm going to turn the generator on.

> *(MATT goes inside, fumbling in the dark on the main rostra, WILL hangs back, shuffling and unsure what to do.)*

WILL: Matthew, best man, where are you?…I need your body warmth…I'm moving forward. *(He bangs his shin.)* I've shinned myself. I've stubbed my shin.

MATT: He's shinned it.

> *(Fumbles his way to join MATT.)*

WILL: Aaah, I am sooo cold.

MATT: I have no sympathy for a man who swaps his coat for a plastic Viking helmet…with one horn.

WILL: I will bring it Matthew. I am capable of bringing it, bitch.

MATT: Why don't you just bring it, dog?

WILL: I will bring it, and when I do bring it I will rain 'it' down on your village, on your neighbourhood, on your kith and kin –

(Behind the screen, NEIL bangs a plastic box next to a mic. providing the noise of the generator firing up. Lights up.)

(WILL and MATT take in their surroundings, impressed.)

MATT: Neil, Neil, Neil. *(To WILL.) This* is bringing it. Here is a man who brings it.

MATT: *(Looking from wall to wall at imaginary paintings and sculptures.)* … Art… Art.

WILL: Art.

MATT: What's with the art Neil?

NEIL: What?

(NEIL joins them on the main rostra, rubbing his hands together in the cold.)

NEIL: It heats up pretty quickly once the generator kicks in. Who wants a drink?

MATT: Tea.

WILL: Beer! Tea.

NEIL: I'll see what I can do. *(NEIL exits, behind the screen again. It is clear this is where the kitchen is represented.)*

MATT: *(Noticing more art.)* Oh, pots!

WILL: *(By now WILL has discovered a fancy stereo and CDs. He turns to look where MATT is.)* Ceramics, Matthew. *Ceramics.*

WILL: Neil, you have a very eclectic CD collection!

NEIL: *(From the kitchen.)* Yeah, put something on.

WILL: Where's the Bob?

MATT: Please no.

WILL: An education, an education. *(Hunting through CDs.)*

NEIL: *(Offstage.)* Will peppermint do?

MATT: Masala Chai is preferable please Neil.

WILL: Jasmine.

NEIL: *(Offstage.)* Yeah, like I said, will peppermint do?

MATT: That'll be lovely, thank you very much.

WILL: *(Finding CD.)* Desire!

NEIL: *(Offstage.)* Yes!!

MATT: Oh god.

WILL: Vintage mid-career Bob.

NEIL: *(Re-entering.)* I mean, who else would rhyme 'kelp' with 'help'?

WILL: This is it, this is what I am trying to tell him. I can't work your machine it doesn't have any buttons. It's too flash, what does it have, sensors?

(NEIL moves in. The stereo is imagined, facing the audience, built into the back wall of the top rostra, a sort of living-room mezzanine level. Both WILL and NEIL are waving their arms ineffectually in front of it to catch a sensor beam.)

WILL: *(Moving off and leaving it to NEIL.)* The word is thrown around a lot but who else besides 'His Bobness' deserves the epithet 'genius' today, who else?

MATT: OK, well…

WILL: No I don't want you to actually…

MATT: Clapton!

WILL: Matthew please…

MATT: Diamond!

WILL: You're testing me here…

(NEIL has given up on the stereo and now has the cordless landline phone in his hands and is dialling.)

MATT: Manilow!

NEIL: That's just rude…

(WILL playfully attacks MATT on the three wooden chairs, which now represent the sofa. NEIL is holding the phone to his ear and awaiting an answer.)

WILL: Matthew, you are my best friend, I love you, but this is starting to get in the way of our relationship.

MATT: Is it?

WILL: Most people get into Dylan in their twenties, what are you now, 35, 36?

MATT: 32!

NEIL: *(Answerphone message.)* Hi, Hvad seyjirdu got, eru Neil her. Eg er med tvo enskur madurinn sem er a 'stag do'. Vid erum a Sumer husid.

(WILL & MATT listen for a moment then lose interest.)

WILL: Just come over, join us.

MATT: I am happy where I am.

(NEIL moves off back into the kitchen so he can hear himself talk.)

WILL: You think you're happy but once you've made the journey.

MATT: But I don't want to travel.

NEIL: …Heyrudu, eg var ad hugsa, kannski er a betteri ef vid hittumst a morgunn, kannski klukkan etlava eda eitthvad?

WILL: You will find true happiness. Do the voice!

MATT: I shan't be doing the voice this evening.

NEIL: …Bara hringdu mig ef thad er a malid. OK, bless.

WILL: Come on, do the voice, you're good at the voice.

MATT: No, I don't want to.

WILL: Do it, do it, do it.

MATT: No, no, no.

WILL: I will kiss you if you don't.

MATT: Why would you –

(WILL moves in.)

MATT: *(Immediately doing his Dylan.)* Yeah. I'm singin' 'bout the wind. All I ever sing about is the wind.

WILL: Yes.

(NEIL re-enters as MATT starts the impression, replaces the phone handset on the mezzanine, by the stepladder and walks round to sit next to MATT on the sofa.)

MATT: I've now done the voice.

WILL: And that's where it starts.

MATT: That's where it stops.

(Small pause.)

WILL: Those other stags we ran into…

NEIL: *(Football chant voice.)* Andy, Andy!

WILL: They all had the Viking helmets but it wasn't consistent with the rest of their outfits. I saw a nun, a Fred Flintstone…

NEIL: Scooby Doo.

WILL: It was just disorganised.

MATT: Ah, unlike somebody's stag do which has been…

NEIL: *(Indulging MATT.)* Very well organised thank you Matthew.

WILL: A triumph.

MATT: Thank you Neil. Gentlemen I call a laminate check, show me your laminates please.

WILL: I lost it.

(NEIL shows his, a small laminated stag itinerary.)

MATT: What?

WILL: It was in my coat!

MATT: Fortunately I have spares for everybody, please be more careful *(Hands over laminate from inside his black bum-bag that remains protectively round his waist at all times.)*

WILL: Thank you Matt, very thorough. *(Now studying the printed reverse of the laminate.)* I have to tell you I didn't have any use for my useful expressions. Although 'Ertu thid med Hopafslatt.'

NEIL: *(Helpfully and swiftly translating.)* 'Do you do a group discount?'

WILL: …could have been useful and 'Help, I have become separated from my group…'

NEIL: 'Vid Vidskilla vid Hopinn.'

WILL: …is becoming increasingly relevant. The phrase I could have done with was 'why after repeated discussions on the subject did I find myself in a strip club'?

MATT: It was ironic! *(Unzipping his little bag again and taking out his BlackBerry.)* I'll have you know, for your father the strip club was a deal-breaker.

WILL: That is a detail I could really do without.

MATT: I'm going to call Swifty, see where they are.

WILL: Yeah, where are they?

NEIL: *(Standing.)* That dance he was doing. I mean, what was that? Can you even call it dancing when you only use one leg?

MATT: 'The Swifty.'

WILL: And he goes round, clockwise.

NEIL: I mean the left leg is going at it quite a bit, but the right leg is sort of nailed to the floor…

MATT: *(On the phone.)* Swifty! Where are you?

WILL: We're there!

MATT: Oh God, listen to this. *(Puts on speakerphone. There is shouting and carnage from the other stags. NEIL and WILL try making contact shouting things like 'where are you' and 'hurry up.' MATT takes it off speakerphone.)* Swifty, are you coming? Hello? He's gone. They're having a good time.

(NEIL has been briefly studying the [imagined] floor to ceiling blind at the front of the main rostra and discovers a small button DSL on the wall. He pushes it. Sound effect, quiet whirring as the blind rises into the ceiling revealing the floor to ceiling glass window/door in front of them that runs along the length of the house. They all look outside. Pause.)

MATT: *(Softly.)* What's out there Neil?

NEIL: All sorts.

MATT: Like what?

NEIL: OK, well, *(Pointing things out through the glass.)* that's the lava field in front of us there, the road along the coast runs behind that. Over there somewhere is the gorge we drove past and that black bit over there is a mountain.

WILL: What black bit? It's all black.

NEIL: Well, the blackest bit.

(There is a rumbling noise that gradually grows, after a couple of seconds the stage they are standing on shakes too. The noise and shaking crescendo and then fade to nothing quickly.)

MATT: What's that?

NEIL: Oh that's just a tremor. Don't worry we get two or three of them a week here.

(NEIL walks DS centre and mimes opening the glass door – accompanying 'shhh' sound effect and goes outside.)

MATT: *(To WILL.)* Just a tremor?

WILL: It's cold, close the door, close the door, close the door, close the door…

(MATT joins NEIL on the veranda and closes door behind him. WILL can no longer be heard from inside the house. Pause.)

NEIL: Hear that? *(MATT listens perplexed.)* The wind has died down.

MATT: Oh yeah.

NEIL: It does that here…just sort of whips up out of nowhere and then disappears just as quickly.

(Both of them look out, hugging themselves against the cold, then looking at the star-filled sky.)

NEIL: It's so clear now. I wonder if you could count them all.

MATT: One, two, three, four…

NEIL: *(Incredulous and amused. Sarcastic.)* Well you'll never count them all on your own, why don't you start at one end and I'll start over here and I'll meet you in the middle?

MATT: One, two…

NEIL: It was a joke.

MATT: Oh right.

(WILL slides open the door. Each time the door is opened or closed there is an accompanying sound effect. Towards the end of the previous exchange he has been shuffling around indoors, attempting to use the furniture to open a bottle of beer.)

WILL: Have you got a bottle opener?

NEIL: It's in the kitchen, try one of the drawers.

(WILL closes door.)

MATT: *(Suddenly sincere.)* Thank you Neil.

NEIL: That's alright. It's here isn't it, might as well use it.

(WILL can be heard rooting through the kitchen behind the screen.)

NEIL: You might see the northern lights if you're lucky.

MATT: Really?

NEIL: You've got more chance the further away from the city you get.

MATT: They're green aren't they?

NEIL: Yeah, well it varies, they're never quite the same twice, sometimes it's just a green streak…

(WILL returns and opens door.)

WILL: Can't find it.

NEIL: *(Takes the bottle, studies for a second, and then twists it open with his hands.)*…Sometimes they illuminate the whole sky. You get great big swirls dancing around. Anyway, fingers crossed.

(WILL closes door, notices hot tub through the window, opens door.)

WILL: What's that?

(WILL closes door.)

NEIL: *(To MATT.)* I see Will's found the hot tub.

MATT: *(Opens door.)* Neil says it's a hot tub.

WILL: It's a hot tub! *(MATT closes door and we stop hearing WILL, who continues to celebrate – dumb show.)*

MATT: *(Indicating the tub, still beneath the dust sheet.)* Can that happen?

NEIL: Yeah, alright, help me get this off would you. *(Takes off the dust sheet revealing the three plastic chairs that become the hot tub. He studies the length of the side of the house.)* There's usually some sort of hose attachment from the kitchen.

MATT: *(Pointing.)* It says 'on' there, Neil. Is that…?

NEIL: Oh yeah.

(Presses the 'on' button on the side of the paint stripper. After a couple of minutes this provides the noise and steam of the tub.)

NEIL: We've only just had it installed, haven't used it yet. It takes a few minutes to fill up. I'll find us something to put on.

(NEIL goes inside behind the screen again. MATT follows inside and leaves the door open. WILL is stripping and singing in the style of gangsta-rap – 'going in the hot tub, with my bitches and my hoes' MATT joins in with singing and stripping.)

WILL: *(Seeing MATT topless but still with his bum bag on.)* This is a good look for you.

MATT: You like this? It just gets better my friend. *(MATT pulls trousers down, he is now in boxers and bum bag, hopping towards WILL with his trousers round his ankles.)*

(NEIL enters just in trunks, with two pairs of matching trunks and towels for the others and gives them out.)

NEIL: Here, try these on.

(WILL and MATT cease posturing and change shyly, NEIL gets in hot tub.)

(WILL and MATT eventually join him. NEIL has discovered the stash of beer either side of the tub, probably in the snow, and is sipping one.)

HOT TUB 1 – MEN

(MATT gets in with bum bag still on. Somewhere along the way, he has acquired the Viking helmet, which now sits on his head.)

MATT: Oh no! Argh!

WILL: You should have laminated the bag.

(NEIL hands out beers.)

NEIL: 'Skal!'

WILL & MATT: *(Incoherent toasts, attempting foreign.)*

(They all relax in tub. There is no room for them to stretch their legs without becoming entangled. They jostle.)

WILL: You go through, I'm going over.

MATT: I want to go through and down.

NEIL: Yeah, I'm not a fan of the leg situation.

(There is a bucket with a small amount of water in it next to the chairs. It is microphoned. Throughout the scene the actors use this to evoke the noises in the tub.)

(Pause.)

WILL: This is a bit disappointing isn't it?

NEIL: *(Joining in the sarcasm.)* Yeah sorry, I'll take you back straight away.

MATT: This is what happens when you stray off laminate.

WILL: Well I want to get back on schedule; I want to be back in a slightly cramped hotel room with 12 other men watching late night TV.

(Beat.)

NEIL: Weirdly they don't have late night TV here.

WILL & MATT: What?!

NEIL: They have an on-screen quiz; background music, picture of a waterfall or something, and true or false questions. 'Satt etha ljuga'.

MATT: 'Satt etha ljuga'?

WILL: Well that's what our rival stag party are doing about now.

NEIL: *(Same football chant as before.)* Andy! Andy!

WILL: Or not. They've probably tied themselves to a barge… on their way to Sweden…

MATT: With a cow.

NEIL: 'Andy, what's the cow doin' here?'

WILL: Where were they from?

NEIL: Sheffield.

MATT: *(Doing his 'northern'.)* Where that there Billy Elliot is from, ain't it Neil?

NEIL: *(Tired of this long-running game.)* No. That's Newcastle.

WILL: Same sort of deal though, right?

NEIL: Very good.

MATT: Do you play in colliery brass band Neil?

WILL: Did you have a pet kestrel Neil?

MATT: Mad for it, mad for it, mad for it, mad for it.

NEIL: *(Turning it round.)* OK, where was all this quality banter when you had a whole rugby league team in front of you. Then it was *(Posh voice.)* 'Yes, we are doctors. My, you're a big chap aren't you... I do admire your tattoo'.

MATT: Did I say that?

(Pause.)

WILL: *(Imitating Sheffield stags.)* Andy! Andy!

NEIL: 'Andy, it's the posh doctors again!'

WILL: *(Stands up and shouts.)* Stag! Stag!

(NEIL joins in the manly whooping and noise which echoes round the wilderness.)

MATT: Shssh, guys please. You'll attract something.

WILL: What were you thinking I might attract exactly, Matthew?

MATT: I don't know...wolves?

WILL: Is it wolves? Are there wolves here?

NEIL: Sort of.

WILL: Sort of wolves.

MATT: How likely are wolves?

NEIL: OK, more likely than a reindeer…less likely than a polar bear.

MATT: A *polar bear*?!

(WILL and MATT both look out to the wilderness, suddenly seeing it in a different light.)

WILL: Seriously, are there polar bears here?

NEIL: Yeah… *(Reacting to general disbelieving noises and snorts.)* Well they're not native obviously but they come over from Greenland, they get separated from the mainland and drift off on the ice. So they bed down and wait till they wash up somewhere…

(Being interrupted.)

MATT: 'Ljuga', please let it be 'ljuga'.

WILL: 'Satt! Satt!

NEIL: It's true!! And sometimes they arrive here… tired, grumpy, very hungry, and they go for the first thing they see…

WILL: They particularly like smooth little men.

NEIL: In Viking helmets.

NEIL: The farmers in the north have shot guns. You're all right as long as you don't make too much noise.

MATT: OK so can we just keep a lid on it please.

(Silence. MATT looks around anxiously.)

NEIL: *(Making MATT jump.)* Aaaaaaaah!

MATT: *(Frightened.)* No! It's a no from me.

NEIL: *(Laughing with WILL.)* I'm going for a slash.

(NEIL exits the hot tub, opens the glass doors, enters the house chuckling, closes them behind him and wanders off behind the screen.)

MATT: *(Looking through guide book, which he takes from his trusty bum bag muttering.)* Pffh! Polar bears!

WILL: It's true! I read about it in the in-flight magazine.

MATT: There's no mention of polar bears in here.

MATT: *(Flicking through pages before coming across something that grabs his attention.)* Ah! Crevice!

WILL: Crevice!

MATT: Look, 'Kingsjungar Crevice', that's our lad. *(Reads from book.)* 'An inland crevice running a criss-cross line of geothermal activity, an hour's drive from Reykjavik… This crevice is only accessible on foot across a hardened lava field… It's famous for being the keeper of the 'Yngling' rocks. Viking tribes from across the country would meet here and legend has it that the initiates of the Jomsviking tribe would dive down to retrieve the rocks in a herculean rite-of-passage…'

WILL: What, this one here?

MATT: Yeah, our boy. *(Noticing the sobering detail.)* Ah. 'In the last 10 years, three Reykjavik youngsters have lost their lives attempting to replicate this heroic act of their forebears.'

(Suddenly there is the sound of something hitting against the window from inside the house, followed by flapping.)

MATT: Jesus…what was that?!

WILL: It's a bird! Bird in the house!

MATT: Oh great.

WILL: Neil, there's a bird, bird in the house! I'll let it out.

MATT: No Will, don't get involved.

WILL: It's fine, I'll just open the door. *(He goes inside.)* Shall I feed it?

MATT: No, that's the last thing you should do.

WILL: Give it some beer?

MATT: No! Neil, Will's antagonising a bird!

(The flapping noise stops. NEIL returns.)

NEIL: What?

WILL: There's a crow.

(They all look up into the rafters.)

WILL: Where's it gone?

NEIL: It's up in the rafters. Leave it, it'll find its own way out eventually.

(Effect as the lights fade to a state like an overexposed negative photograph & a soundscape of building wind. NEIL and WILL walk back to the hot tub and sit. All three place more beer bottles on the wooden deck behind them. The noise crescendo then stops abruptly. It is clear from relaxed attitudes and the increase in bottles that there has been a TIMESHIFT.)

(Mid-conversation.)

WILL: That's my point, I don't think men and women should co-habit before marriage because they zap our strength.

MATT: OK, come on, good to get this out before the big day.

WILL: But then we zap theirs...so it evens out.

NEIL: What kind of ceremony is it?

MATT: It's pagan, a pagan ceremony.

WILL: It's humanist.

MATT: We're going pagan.

WILL: Humanist! Chloe's parents are quite religious and we are not so much so –

MATT: It's *near* a church.

WILL: So we're having it in a field.

MATT: *Right next to* a church.

WILL: You get a bit of both…it's humanist *(Responding to their ridicule.)* …what? I'm into it.

WILL: Actually, I'm not sure.

MATT: Well, talk to her.

WILL: Maybe, maybe.

> *(TIMESHIFT repeats. MATT and NEIL swap places in the tub, more beer bottles behind them and WILL is on the veranda.)*

WILL: *(Standing in the snow, freezing. They are playing the game of who can stand in the snow the longest.)* – 16, 17, 18, 19.

MATT: 6, 7, 8, 9.

WILL: You're counting slower…it's so cold, it's so cold.

> *(Jumps back in.)*

MATT: Oh dear that is poor.

> *(NEIL smiling and enjoying their discomfort a little.)*

> *(TIMESHIFT – shorter than before.)*

MATT: *(Showing his hairline.)* A thumbnail's width gone, in the last five years. I'm having surgery on this. Going to have it taken out the back and popped in the front.

WILL: It looks good. You look good.

NEIL: *(Picking a hair out of the tub.)* Is this one of yours?

MATT: Indeed it is, thank you Neil. *(Taking it from him.)* I will re-attach.

WILL: Go on Neil.

NEIL: *(Picking up a conversation they were obviously having until MATT's hair crisis diverted them.)* Oh, right, well it's sort of a tourist site now and you're not really allowed to do it…but what you do is you dive down into the crevice, underneath the hard lava, swimming along with the lava above you and you get a rock. But it's dark and, unless you know, you don't realise you can swim on and come up for air, so they turn around and try to swim back, and you can't hold your breath that long. They found a teenager down there. It was in the news, last year I think.

(Pause.)

MATT: Let's do it.

(They all pause, MATT puts his hand in for a group pledge.)

Are we in?

(No one responds, they laugh.)

(TIMESHIFT: Lights & sound as before. They all get out of the tub and make their way back to the positions they were in last time they were the Jomsvikings, DSL next to the veranda decking.)

JOMSVIKING QUEUE 2

(Viking waltz music fades up with the lights.)

(MATT is now on the veranda. The other two remain on the floor next to it; they are a little nearer the beheadings than before, all with their arms crossed at the wrist.)

NEIL: Who's that then?

MATT: It's Gisli.

ALL: *(Repeat of the goalkeeper running up to take a goal kick football crowd chant.)* Whoooooooooah! Yes!

MATT: Finally. He's swinging through now.

NEIL: *(Nodding.)* He's letting the axe do the work.

(Beat.)

WILL: Tord! Tord!

(Wind blows. MATT faces out as before. WILL and NEIL react as before.)

WILL: Mate, it's your hair!

MATT: Behave.

NEIL: *(Quietly. Very conversational.)* So you got any plans when you get up there?

WILL: Yes, I'm going to ask for the axe in the face. Like my dad.

NEIL: Right.

WILL: Kind of a signature.

NEIL: Yeah, family tradition kind of thing.

MATT: That's classy, that's nice.

WILL: You?

NEIL: I'm going to go beheading, but I think I'll have enough muscle memory to get my arms round the axe man and give him a *(He gestures strangulation and then neck break.)*

MATT: What, headless?

NEIL: Well, I'm not going to move first am I, where's the fun in that? Yes. Let me know how I get on.

WILL: I shall my friend, I shall tell you in Valhalla. What about you, Eidur? Gonna put your hair up for a start?

MATT: I'm having it down actually.

(Tension.)

WILL: Sure, you'll have it down till the execution but then you'll put it up.

MATT: No, I'm going to keep it down.

NEIL: Don't be a dick.

MATT: What?

WILL: Well you're going to get blood and mud all over it.

NEIL: It'll be ruined. You can't do that to us!

MATT: It's my hair.

WILL/NEIL: But it belongs to all of us, it's famed across the land as a symbol of the tribe.

MATT: It's attached to my head!

NEIL: *(To WILL softly.)* Leave it, we'll work on him later.

    (Beat.)

WILL: *(Under his breath.)* Selfish prick.

MATT: What did he say?

WILL: Do you want to go?

MATT: Tell him, I will bring it, believe me.

    (They verbally spar. NEIL silences them.)

NEIL: *(Shouting.)* I have got a hangover!!

    (Beat.)

WILL: *(Starting chant.)* 'We are the Jomsvikings, we are the Jomsvikings!'

NEIL/MATT: 'Joms!'

WILL: 'We are the Jomsvikings, we are the Jomsvikings'

NEIL/MATT: 'Joms!!'

    (The chant continues. With the help of a sound recording, the rest of the queue joins in.)

    (They challenge the audience directly, as if they are the Norwegian public.)

WILL: Finally a bit of atmosphere! Call this an execution?

MATT: It's like a library in here, Norway!

WILL: Back in Iceland, we know how to do an execution. Nine simultaneous beheadings!

NEIL: Put all the bodies in a boat, burn it, send it out to sea. *That's* an execution!

WILL: What have you got? Your king!

NEIL: *(Sneering.)* What's he here for anyway?

MATT: Wants to see how brave we are, doesn't he?

NEIL: Fair enough.

> *(The sound of the queue chanting peters out.)*

> *(Beat.)*

> *(Bird flutter noise.)*

NEIL: *(Looking out front, over the audience's heads.)* Oh look. Odin's little messenger, doesn't miss a trick does he? Tell him we'll be with him in five minutes.

MATT: You'll be lucky with this guy swinging the axe.

NEIL: Tell him we'll be with him in five days!

> *(They laugh. The bird flies off.)*

NEIL: *(The queue is finally moving.)* Oh, here we go.

> *(MATT moves up queue, NEIL stands on his hair.)*

MATT: Ow! Ow!

> *(Laughter.)*

NEIL: Well then, L'Oréal, tie it up!

MATT: I'm having it down!

> *(The queue stops moving once all three are on the veranda. They face out.)*

WILL: Tord! Tord!

> *(TIMESHIFT – WILL and MATT return to the tub.)*

HOT TUB 2 – STRANGE ART

(NEIL is rolling in snow, DSL in front of the veranda. MATT & WILL watching.)

MATT: No, Neil.

> *(NEIL gets back in tub.)*

MATT: Explain yourself.

NEIL: You do it three times actually, snow, hot tub, snow, hot tub, snow, hot tub, getting further away each time, then shower.

(NEIL goes for the second one, offstage through audience.)

WILL: Watch out polar bears.

(Pause.)

WILL: I am in a womb Matthew. Best man, please can you arrange for this situation to continue until further notice.

MATT: I'm afraid that won't be possible. Oh, I see a chink of light, and what's this? Forceps! A big push, this is it, come on, out you get.

WILL: *(During this.)* No. Please. One more beer. You're the placenta. Feed me beer.

MATT: Placenta beer? OK, one more.

(MATT goes into house. Throughout the following, he remains onstage and notices something that grabs his attention. He moves onto the mezzanine level trying to get the stereo to work then stares at the 'wall' just above head height facing off left.)

(NEIL returns and gets into tub.)

WILL: Neil, kids; discuss. What's it like having a kid?

NEIL: *(Pause. NEIL looks forlornly out into the wilderness/audience.)* It's like having some very heavy shopping. All the time. But good shopping, you know, expensive shopping.

WILL: Marriage. Discuss.

(Beat. NEIL looks at WILL. NEIL gets out of tub and leaves up through the audience.)

(MATT returns to tub with beer.)

MATT: One placenta beer sir.

WILL: You are a good best man.

MATT: Have you seen the case thing? On the wall. The art.

WILL: What?

MATT: There's three, sort of beavers, floating in, you know, formaldehyde, looking at you.

WILL: What?

MATT: They're identical. *(He demonstrates their shape.)* I think they're foetuses; three of them. All staring.

WILL: *(Perplexed and not sure if it is a wind-up.)* This I must see. This better be good, I'm getting out of the womb for this.

(WILL opens the door and goes into the house.)

WILL: Where are they?

MATT: Over in the corner. On the wall.

(WILL closes the door and goes over and onto the mezzanine level.)

(NEIL returns to tub.)

MATT: What are your three friends?

(Beat.)

MATT: The art.

NEIL: What?

MATT: In the case. On the wall. Are they beavers?

(WILL runs silently DS to the door, his mouth open. As he opens the door he gives voice to the scream he is emitting.)

WILL: Ah! Nasty, nasty, nasty man! What are they?

MATT: See!!

(They compare notes.)

WILL: Ergh…downy! They're looking at you…

MATT: I know!

WILL: It's like at the…er…at the…

MATT: The Hunterian.

WILL: Right, exactly! The Hunterian museum.

(NEIL takes this opportunity to get out.)

NEIL: I'm going for a shower.

(NEIL exits behind the screen again, taking a towel with him, stopping to discreetly look at the offending art.)

OUTING OF NEIL

WILL: Hirst's gerbil phase?

(Pause. MATT lowers his voice and glances nervously inside first.)

MATT: Will… Will… This is weird.

WILL: *(Joining the whispering game without knowing why.)* It's *so* weird.

MATT: No, listen. I just asked Neil, 'What are they.' And he was like, 'what'? *(Mimics NEIL looking confused.)* I don't know.

WILL: *(Clueless.)* Yeah.

MATT: If you'd bought that, or had it commissioned, or done it yourself I don't know, then, you'd…

(WILL just stares.)

MATT: *(Grasping for the evidence as it occurs to him and starts to fall into place.)* No, right, when we found the hot tub, yeah, who found the switch?

WILL: *(Shrugs.)* He did, you did, who did?

MATT: I did. He was off round the side looking for a hose. And when we arrived, who found the key?

WILL: You did.

MATT: Yes, under the rock, he was like 'where did I put it?'

WILL: And he's supposed to be this big Dylan freak but he's only got one album. 'Desire'.

MATT: Right. Look, you know him through John, right?

(Beat. Stillness.)

WILL: *(Barely above a whisper.)* I thought *you* knew him through John.

MATT: *(Whispering also.)* I don't know him.

WILL: Well I don't know him.

MATT: Does John know him?

(Beat.)

MATT: This is not his house!

(Beat.)

MATT: It's not his house!!

WILL: It's not his house!

MATT: It's not his house!

WILL: OK wait, wait, wait.

(They both stand, on the verge of panic, talking a little louder now, lines overlapping.)

MATT: We need to go. Let's just get in the car and drive…

WILL: Wait, we need to get in the car… Keys, where are his keys?

MATT: Keys Will, KEYS!

(NEIL, wrapped in a towel, makes his way back through the house and opens the door onto the veranda.)

MATT & WILL: *(Instantly reacting, sitting, trying to be cool.)* Hey yeah.

(NEIL takes his time, closes the door, takes off his towel, trunks still on underneath. Carefully he folds the towel and places it back on the veranda before picking his way back to his seat in the hot tub.)

(WILL and MATT glance at each other.)

(Long pause as they relax in the tub.)

NEIL: It's hard to leave isn't it.

(WILL & MATT eye each other again, alarmed.)

(NEIL looks to them.)

WILL & MATT: Yep. Yeah. Hey.

WILL: *(Awkwardly.)* So this is all yours is it Neil?

NEIL: Yeah, erm, down as far as the river I think. I'm not really sure, I should find out I suppose.

WILL: And the art, what are you, a collector?

NEIL: No my uncle was, he left it all to mum so when she went, it sort of came with the house I guess, I don't really know what to do with it all.

MATT: *(Going for the direct approach.)* This is not your house, is it, Neil?

(Pause. NEIL glances at them both, weighing up his options. Something in their looks tells him he has to own up.)

NEIL: *(Looking away out into the wilderness for the confession.)* Well…

(Beat.)

WILL: Where are we, Neil?

(Pause.)

NEIL: I'm not really sure.

MATT & WILL: *(Standing up.)* Oh god, this is great.

MATT AND WILL ATTEMPT TO TAKE CONTROL

MATT: Right, OK, OK. *(He gets out of tub and stands on the veranda.)*

WILL: Wait.

MATT: I'm not staying in there.

(WILL gets out too.)

WILL: *(To NEIL.)* You are driving us back to Reykjavik.

NEIL: It's alright.

WILL: It's not alright. It's a very long way from alright. It's about as far from alright as it's possible to go.

MATT: If not further, actually.

WILL: Matthew, please.

(NEIL goes to get up. MATT & WILL retreat. NEIL sits down in defeat.)

WILL: I'm going to get the keys.

(WILL goes into house and comes straight back.)

WILL: Where are the keys?

NEIL: They're in my jeans.

MATT: They're in his jeans.

WILL: Matthew, I think I heard him.

MATT: They're in his jeans.

(WILL goes further into the house, then comes back.)

WILL: Where are your jeans?

NEIL: They're in the bedroom.

MATT: They're in the bedroom.

WILL: I think I heard that, do you think I heard that?

MATT: Yes, yes!

(WILL goes off into bedroom, US behind the screen.)

(Pause.)

NEIL: Get back in the tub at least, you're going to freeze to death out there.

(MATT thinks about this, then gets into tub very warily.)

(WILL returns.)

WILL: Right, I've got… Matthew! What the fuck are you doing?

MATT: I got in! He told me!

WILL: We're going! We're going!

(MATT gets out of tub.)

WILL: Come on, let's go.

NEIL: What now?

WILL: Yes now.

NEIL: We can't go now, look how much we've had to drink. I can't drive. It's not safe!

WILL: Right, I'll drive.

MATT: No, no, you can't drive.

WILL: What?

MATT: If anything happens, that's it, we are struck off, game over.

(WILL thinks.)

NEIL: Come on, it's OK, we'll tidy up –

MATT: Right, I'll start tidying up.

(MATT goes into house.)

WILL: Matt.

NEIL: Look it's not such a big deal here, people leave their houses open. I've fucked up, I'm sorry. We'll tidy up, no one will even know we've been here I promise. I'll get some sleep, I'll sober up and then we'll get breakfast and I'll drive us back. OK?

(WILL goes inside.)

(MATT arrives back from behind the screen with bin bag for recycling beer bottles.)

WILL: Right, here's what we're going to do, we'll sober up, and then we'll drive back –

MATT: Where does he put... *(Moving outside, WILL desperately trailing after him.)* Neil where do you put your recycling... it's not even his house!

(MATT turns around and heads back inside. WILL follows.)

WILL: What...the fucking recycling?!

MATT: Oh god, it's coming on.

WILL: What's the matter.

MATT: It's my head, my head.

(MATT sits down on the sofa.)

WILL: Get your stick.

(WILL fiddles in MATT's bum bag.)

MATT: I can get my own stick!

(MATT applies a soothing menthol stick to his temples.)

(WILL closes the door.)

(There is a dumb show argument – pointing, accusing, MATT, head between his knees, breathes deeply.)

(WILL opens door, stands in front of NEIL furious, shuts door again.)

(He massages MATT's shoulders.)

(NEIL opens door and enters house, unseen by the others. He now has vodka bottle in his hand which he absent-mindedly picked up from amongst the beer around the hot tub.)

WILL & MATT: Whoah, whoah!

WILL: What is this, Neil? What were you doing flashing your money all over Reykjavik?

(He snatches vodka from NEIL.)

NEIL: I know, I'm sorry. I just wanted us to have fun.

MATT: Fun was scheduled, thank you. *(He throws laminates at NEIL from inside the bum bag.)*

WILL: How was driving two hours out of Reykjavik and breaking into someone's house connected to that? Whose place is this anyway?

NEIL: I don't know! They should never have been built; the land is sacred round here. They're all owned by rich foreigners. I knew the place would be empty at this time of year.

WILL: So you've done this before? This is something you do?

NEIL: Yes. No.

WILL: Do you know what, I don't really care, just get some sleep and drive us back.

NEIL: I came here once with my wife, my ex-wife, we had a really nice time, at least I thought it was here but it must have been one of the other ones, I don't know, it's dark.

WILL: Right, I'm really sorry that you've broken into the wrong house! But that's not really our problem is it?

(Beat.)

WILL: Just go. Just get some sleep.

(NEIL heads dejectedly off to bedroom.)

MATT: Whoah, no, you're sleeping here Neil, please.
(Indicating the sofa.)

WILL: You're sleeping here.

(NEIL makes his way over. They move away from him, watching him sit on the sofa.)

WILL: You're sleeping here until…well how much have we drunk? Four, five beers?

(MATT and WILL talk privately.)

MATT: Play it safe; eight, nine.

WILL: How many pints is that?

MATT: No it's units. 1.5…

WILL: OK, so that's…

NEIL: It doesn't matter, it's more lenient here, everything is more lenient here. You only get eight years for murder.

(Beat. NEIL puts his head in his hands as MATT and WILL digest this.)

MATT: Five hours, let's say five hours.

WILL: You'll sleep for five hours, as long as you drink plenty of water.

MATT: Yes, water.

WILL: OK?

(NEIL doesn't respond. Head still in hands.)

WILL: Neil?

NEIL: *(Composes himself and looks up at them.)* I'm sorry. I'm ok now… *(He bursts into tears.)*

(Pause.)

WILL: Now this.

NEIL: I've fucked up. You know, I just saw you guys…

MATT: No…

NEIL: I wanted to get out of the city for a bit.

MATT: *(Gently.)* OK Neil, we just want you to get your head down, get some sleep, and then we can all drive on back to Reykjavik and we'll –

WILL: *(Shouting.)* You sleep for 5 hours and drive back to Reykjavik! That's what's happening!

(NEIL lies down. MATT covers him with towel.)

MATT: Sleep well Neil.

(WILL shoots him a look. MATT responds.)

MATT: What?

THE TRAGIC MYTH OF THUNKATAR AND YGDRASIL

(Viking waltz music.)

WILL: *(Addressing audience.)* One day, up in Asgaard, Thor lost his famous hammer.

MATT: *(As THOR.)* Where's my bloody hammer now?!

WILL: Inconsolable, he spent his evenings drinking in the famous Raven Café. *(He switches on the Dot Matrix. 'Raven Café' scrolls across it at regular intervals.)* Come on Thor, that's last orders, time to go home.

(MATT puts a dust sheet around him as his cloak.)

MATT: No, no…tell me, how do I look?

WILL: You look fine. Maybe not as good as Odin.

MATT: Urgh.

(NEIL, as LOKI, wakes on the sofa in the bar.)

MATT: Loki!

WILL: Loki, get out of here you're barred!

NEIL: What?

MATT: No, he's with me. Loki, dance with me, come on.

(They dance.)

(WILL exits behind the screen with recycling and switches off Raven Café sign.)

NEIL: Let's get you home. How's the wife by the way?

MATT: She's fine. Actually Loki, it's anything but fine –

(Odin's RAVEN appears.)

MATT: Never mind.

(RAVEN disappears.)

NEIL: I heard about your hammer. *(Glancing discreetly at the vodka bottle which is hidden under the wooden chairs/sofa.)*

MATT: Can't bloody find it anywhere.

NEIL: I probably shouldn't say anything.

MATT: Now, come on, what do you know?

NEIL: *(Very reluctant.)* I'm trying not to spread rumours.

MATT: Tell me, Loki, or I will fuck you up!

NEIL: There's this giant down on Earth – Thunkatar.

> *(WILL as the Giant THUNKATAR appears from behind the screen.)*

MATT: Thunkatar?

NEIL: Yes, he's got your hammer. Go and check it out.

MATT: Thank you, Loki.

> *(THUNKATAR's footsteps echo as he walks. He towers above the model house, intrigued.)*

> *(THOR exits behind the screen.)*

> *(LOKI picks up THOR's hammer [the vodka bottle] and lobs it down to Earth. It hits THUNKATAR on the head and he catches it and inspects it.)*

> *(NEIL becomes YGDRASIL, the giantess.)*

YGDRASIL: Thunkatar, my darling!

THUNKATAR: Oh Ygdrasil, just days now till our wedding. And guess what?

YGDRASIL: What?

THUNKATAR: I have a present for you.

YGDRASIL: You've had dancing lessons?

THUNKATAR: No. I've got a little hammer.

YGDRASIL: Oh.

THUNKATAR: And I'm going to have it melted down by the dwarf blacksmiths to make a ring for you, for our wedding day.

YGDRASIL: A ring! How romantic. How's the poem?

THUNKATAR: The wedding day poem? Going extremely well.

YGDRASIL: All fourteen stanzas?

THUNKATAR: Ah yes, I meant to talk to you about that…

YGDRASIL: Take me!

THUNKATAR: What now?

YGDRASIL: Yes! Fly over this valley and take me in your arms!

THUNKATAR: I'm coming my sweet.

(THUNKATAR prepares himself.).

YGDRASIL: No, no, we must wait.

(MATT enters.)

MATT: *(To audience.)* So Thor flew down to Earth, to reclaim his hammer.

(LOKI blows THOR and his cloak with leaf blower to simulate his flying.)

THOR: *(To LOKI.)* Let it do its own thing.

THUNKATAR: *(Practising his wedding poem.)* 'Your hair is like a mountain stream…your hair – '

THOR: Excuse me? Hello? Down here! It's me, Thor.

(THOR is centre stage and looking up steeply at the giant when he talks.)

THUNKATAR: *(Confused, looking down at his feet.)* I can't hear you little man. Hold on.

(He bends to pick THOR up and places him on his open palm where he finally recognises the god.)

THUNKATAR: Thor!

THOR: Yes, it's me, Thor.

THUNKATAR: Sorry I didn't recognise you. Oh I've ruffled up your cloak –

(NEIL as LOKI blows the cloak with the leaf blower.)

THOR: Leave it. Now, someone's told me you've got my famous hammer, so, come on.

(Pause.)

THUNKATAR: No.

THOR: You haven't?

THUNKATAR: No, no. I don't know where you got that idea.

THOR: Well Loki…Loki said.

THUNKATAR: Well if Loki told you what can you expect? He's famously duplicitous.

THOR: I'm sorry Thunkatar. I'm going through a funny time at the moment. It's my wife you see –

THUNKATAR: Bye Thor.

(He drops THOR who flies back Asgaard.)

(THOR lands back next to LOKI.)

LOKI: Well of course he'd say he hasn't got it.

THOR: You're up to your tricks again!

LOKI: I'm not. I swear. Trust me!

(WILL picks up a dust sheet, puts it on and becomes ODIN crossing the stage in a glorious cape.)

ODIN: Hello Thor.

THOR: Odin.

LOKI: Now that's how you wear a cloak.

THOR: How does he do that? *(Back to the task.)* Right, you're coming down to Earth with me, and we are going to sort this out.

LOKI: Alright.

(They fly back to earth and spy THUNKATAR inspecting the hammer, which he then puts in his pocket.)

LOKI: See, that's your hammer isn't it?

THOR: You're right. But how do I get it back?

THUNKATAR: 'Your hair is like a mountain stream…'

LOKI: Ah yes, he's trying to write a poem for his wedding, but he's terrible. You help him and I'll climb up the inside of his trunks and get your hammer back. Go.

THUNKATAR: 'Your hair is like a mountain stream…'

THOR: Excuse me, it's me again, Thor.

THUNKATAR: Thor, is that you?

THOR: Yes, yes.

(THUNKATAR picks THOR up.)

THOR: No, we don't have to, urgh.

THUNKATAR: The thing is Thor, I'm extremely busy, I'm writing a poem for my wedding day you see.

THOR: Well that's why I'm here.

THUNKATAR: Oh yes?

THOR: I thought I could help you finish it off?

THUNKATAR: Well as a matter fact I could use a little help.

(LOKI makes noises into the DSL microphone, as he climbs up the giant's leg to get to his pocket.)

(THUNKATAR looks down towards his trunks and swings his hips.)

LOKI: Stop swinging that thing around! Aaah!

THOR: Thunkatar, the poem!

THUNKATAR: Well this is what I've got so far. 'Your hair is like a mountain stream…'

LOKI: *(Meaning the hammer.)* Got it!

THUNKATAR: And that's it actually. Can you help?

THOR: OK… 'I want to fish in it? And catch some…sea bream?'

THUNKATAR: Good, a good start. Now –

THOR: OK Thunkatar, must be off. That's great.

THUNKATAR: Wait Thor, it's supposed to be fourteen stanzas!

(THOR and LOKI fly back to Asgaard, where LOKI presents him with his hammer.)

LOKI: There you go, Thor.

THOR: Thank you, Loki! I misjudged you, I apologise.

LOKI: That's alright. *(Walking off mischievously.)* Next time don't leave things lying around in bars. Bye Thor.

THOR: What? Loki!

NEIL: *(As narrator, whilst putting on a dust sheet as a wedding dress and veil to become IGDRASIL.)* Soon, the big day arrived and all that remained was for the giants to go through the formality of asking the god's permission for their marriage.

(THUNKATAR joins IGDRASIL on the veranda, now an altar. They both look skywards towards THOR.)

THUNKATAR: Hello Thor.

THOR: *(USC on the ladder, reigning and godly.)* Hello. Right. State who you are and why you are here.

THUNKATAR: You know me, it's Thunkatar! And Ygdrasil.

THOR: Ah, yes.

THUNKATAR: We're here to ask the god's permission for our marriage. It's a mere formality as you know, but if you just say yes we'll move along.

THOR: It's a no from me.

(THUNKATAR is open-mouthed in amazement. YGDRASIL takes up her veil, furious.)

THUNKATAR: Thor, I don't think you understand, nobody has ever been denied permission.

THOR: Still no.

THUNKATAR: What?

YGDRASIL: Thunkatar, do something.

(THUNKATAR cries. YGDRASIL protests.)

THOR: There are repercussions when you take things that don't belong to you. Be gone.

NEIL: *(As narrator.)* So Thunkatar wandered the earth for all eternity composing bad poetry no one would ever hear.

THUNKATAR: *(Footsteps echoing forlornly. He stops.)* 'There was a young women called Ygdrasil…' Oh fuck it.

NEIL: And Ygdrasil cried so much her tears made a new mountain. And Loki was banished to earth until the gods could work out what to do with him.

(WILL and MATT return to hot tub. NEIL returns to the sofa and lies down. Viking waltz fades out.)

AN UNCOMFORTABLE TRUTH EMERGES/NEIL LEAVES

(Calm. Time has moved on. MATT has the guidebook open. WILL is pointing out over the audience into the wilderness towards the mountain referred to earlier.)

WILL: And what's that one, is that in there?

MATT: That is Mount Ygdrasil. Means mountain of tears.

(WILL and MATT stand and look inside, like meerkats, to check on NEIL.)

WILL: OK so he sleeps for another couple of hours.

MATT: One more hour.

WILL: One hour.

MATT: And then we can get going.

(They laugh at the madness of it.)

MATT: God I'm hungry!

WILL: What have you got on in the next couple of weeks? Aren't you thinking of taking an ITU job or something?

MATT: Yeah, well, it's still an option.

WILL: Why? You'd be mad to leave.

MATT: I know…it's going all right; my boss is really old-school, lets me just get on with it on my own…even in big cases.

WILL: Yeah, great!

(Pause.)

WILL: …and you're doing really well; I've heard fantastic things about your work…

MATT: From who?

WILL: From Melouish.

MATT: Oh god…don't listen to what that guy says.

WILL: No!…an extremely glowing review about some paediatric arrest that you managed to rescue…

MATT: I was assisting…

(Pause.)

WILL: …you know in many ways I'd rather be doing something like what you're doing…

MATT: OK you don't have to –

WILL: No seriously, it turns out the 'surgical fraternity' really are the back-bitey competitive knobs everyone said they would be.

MATT: Yeah, yeah.

WILL: Plus apparently my life expectancy if I retire at 65 is 2 years…

MATT: You don't have to do this routine…it's cool. I'm not a surgeon; you are. It just worked out like this. Luck.

(Pause.)

WILL: Well sorry anyway…

MATT: OK.

WILL: …I probably could have said something to prof at the time that might've helped you get on the rotation but…he was so into research backgrounds, I don't think it would have swung anything…anyway it's worked out so…

(Pause.)

MATT: Right…I thought you did say something.

WILL: Yeah, well I did…

MATT: You did?

WILL: Well no, I didn't…

MATT: Did you or didn't you?

WILL: Matt don't! I know what you're talking about…

MATT: What?

WILL: When we chatted at that party.

MATT: At Fiona's yes.

WILL: Yeah at Fi's, and I said I would 'have a think' about people I could chat to –

MATT: No. No, what you said was, Will, and I quote – 'I'll see what I can do'. Three times.

WILL: Yes!

MATT: …you put your hand around my shoulder… 'I'll see what I can do'… You left me in no doubt , Will, what you meant… 'I'll see what I can do.'

WILL: Yes! 'I'll see what I can do', I'll see what I can do'. That's what I did; I saw –

MATT: Saw what?

WILL: Well ultimately…nothing. I didn't think I could help.

MATT: Hmmmm.

WILL: Matt don't!

(MATT gets out of the tub and enters the house.)

WILL: Matt, what are you doing?

(MATT picks up vodka and drinks from it. He checks on NEIL and sees the beavers on the wall. He goes over and mimes taking the beaver art case off the wall and comes back to the tub, maintaining the shape he is supposed to be carrying.)

WILL: *(Whisper.)* Matt, what are you doing? Put it back.

MATT: So, me and my three friends have come for a little apology.

WILL: Matthew, please, these genuinely freak me out.

(WILL jumps out of the tub and runs across the decking. MATT follows.)

WILL: What are you doing?

MATT: We'll start with Clive on the end.

WILL: What?

MATT: Look Clive in the eye and tell him you are sorry. Go on.

WILL: *(Reluctantly.)* Sorry.

MATT: Good. Now Wendy in the middle.

WILL: Sorry.

MATT: Damian, far end.

WILL: Sorry.

MATT: OK. That's it. That's all we wanted.

WILL: Fine, now put them back. It's probably extremely expensive.

(WILL gets back in the tub. MATT hovers with the case.)

MATT: No…I think I'll just…

WILL: Inside. Put them inside.

(MATT puts the beaver art case on the decking, next to the tub. We hear a thud.)

MATT: There.

(MATT gets in tub.)

WILL: Can you move it, they're looking at me. Twist it.

MATT: They're just being sociable.

(Pause. Indoors NEIL wakes up and sits up on the sofa.)

MATT: …I know why.

WILL: You know why what?

MATT: Why you didn't say anything.

WILL: Look Matt –

(NEIL notices the car key sitting on the sofa beside him. He picks it up, stands and moves slowly towards the tub as the two are arguing outside.)

MATT: …'cause you always have to be that little bit better don't you….if I'm here *(Indicates.)* you've got to be here *(Higher level.)* doing a bit better…don't you?…

(NEIL exits.)

WILL: Matt –

MATT: *(Remembering, laughing. WILL protesting.)* …there you were, hanging out with Prof, daddy's friend let's not forget…all you had to do was put in a word –

WILL: Matt –

MATT: And fuck off about it not making a difference. …I mean it's cool. You know whatever. I'm fine; anaesthetist, whatever…but it just seems weird that it's so important to you…

WILL: *(Exasperated.)*...No, Matt –

MATT: Well why then? why didn't you say something?

WILL: Look –

MATT: Why!? See you can't say anything...

> *(Slaps WILL, but it all seems very cheerful/passive-aggressive.)*

> Why! Why! WHY! WHY!

WILL: Because you're not good enough.

> *(Pause.)*

> And how would that make me look?

> *(Pause.)*

> That's come out wrong...

> *(Pause.)*

> *(MATT picks up a beer bottle and clinks it.)*

MATT: Ladies and Gentlemen, I'm Matthew, Will's best man. I'd like to talk about the first time I met Will. We were 8 years old. And one of the first things he said to me was 'I'm going to take you under my wing'. And he did. So much so he also took my homework, my dinner money and all of my girlfriends!

> *(NEIL enters the space dressed now, approaches the model and takes the car, lit by the torch. During the following sequence NEIL manipulates events invisibly, somehow supernatural.)*

> *(A car is heard leaving.)*

WILL: That's Neil.

MATT: What? Where's Neil?

> *(They look out into the space where the car would be disappearing.)*

WILL: He's gone. 'Cause we weren't bloody watching him!

MATT: Neil!

> *(WILL goes into the kitchen.)* Neil! *(He comes back.)* He's gone.

MATT: Why's he gone?

WILL: Where's your phone?

MATT: It's in my pouch.

WILL: Where's your pouch?

MATT: Where's my pouch? It's there.

(MATT gathers his bum bag and starts to put it on.)

WILL: You don't have to put it on! Get the phone. Get John.

(MATT fiddles with his phone.)

MATT: John, John.

WILL: Scroll down!

MATT: I'm scrolling! There's John.

(WILL snatches the phone.)

WILL: There's no reception.

(He goes outside. NEIL is waiting stage left, watching, invisible.)

WILL: *(His ear to the phone.)* It's calling.

MATT: Talk to John.

WILL: Answer machine!

MATT: Oh God. Tell John.

WILL: Hi John. It's Will and Matt.

MATT: *(Shouting.)* Hi John, I'm with Will. It's Matt here.

WILL: Matthew, please.

(Pushes him inside.)

MATT: Bye John. I'll get our clothes –

(WILL closes door on him.)

WILL: Hi John, we came with Neil to his house but it turns out it isn't his house. We thought you and Swifty were behind us.

(The phone cuts out. WILL wanders down the side of the house in search of better reception.)

(Inside the house, the RAVEN begins to attack MATT; NEIL provides the sound of the bird flapping on the DSL microphone – MATT & RAVEN dumb show.)

WILL: John, continuation of message; I think the last one cut out. I've come with Matt out to the mountains.

(He steps back onto the terrace. MATT runs into the closed door. NEIL makes the noise of the impact. JOHN is phoning. NEIL turns on the microwave SL to cook hotdogs.)

WILL: He's calling, John's calling. John, hi!

(MATT emerges bleeding from his nose. WILL sees him. NEIL calmly walks round the back and replaces the car on the model then walks back DSL.)

WILL: Aaaah!

MATT: Aaaah! Help John! I've been attacked!

WILL: *(Into phone.)* Matthew's bleeding, he's been attacked by the guy from the club!

MATT: Please! We've been abandoned John! Save us!

WILL: John? John!? Shit. I'm going to phone him on the landline.

(He gives MATT the phone.)

MATT: Be careful. It's in there.

(MATT tries to find reception.)

WILL: *(From inside.)* I need the number!

MATT: There's no reception.

WILL: *(Comes back outside.)* I need the number.

MATT: There's no bloody reception!

(MATT lobs phone into wilderness.)

WILL: What are you doing?! We need that phone!

MATT: I know!

WILL: *(Kicks beaver case, which smashes. NEIL provides the sound effect.)* Aaah!

MATT: No! Oh god.

(The smell of the formaldehyde kicks in.)

WILL: It's fine, it's fine.

(WILL tries to scrape the beavers and their goo off the terrace.)

(He slips over into it. They are both gagging a little.)

(NEIL takes out the hot dogs and adds ketchup.)

MATT: No!

WILL: Get it off me! Get the beaver thing off me!

MATT: Hold still, I'll flick it off!

(He flicks it with his toe into the unknown. WILL is going crazy and kicking frantically.)

(MATT falls on top of WILL and they writhe around together.)

MATT: Just scrape it off.

(WILL's attempts to get up but then falls face down in the goo. He elbows MATT in the nose.)

MATT: Oh god, it hurts so much.

HOT DOGS/ NORTHERN LIGHTS/ WILL LEAVES

(During the commotion NEIL has returned and is standing on the edge of the terrace, holding hot dogs They see him.)

WILL: Where the hell have you been?

NEIL: I went to get breakfast.

(MATT and WILL rise.)

WILL: Oh so now there's a café next door is there?

NEIL: No there's a farm just down the road, she's a really nice lady. She makes me a hot dog sometimes if I'm in the area.

WILL: You were supposed to be lying on the sofa until we told you –

MATT: You were under house arrest.

WILL: House arrest.

NEIL: I thought we said I was going to get breakfast and then we were going to go.

WILL: Well why didn't you tell us?

NEIL: I tried to, you were in the middle of a row or something.

MATT: You still should have said something.

NEIL: Would you have let me go if I did?

WILL & MATT: No.

NEIL: Well then.

WILL: It's not a good argument.

(Beat. They eat the hot dogs over the following dialogue.)

MATT: These are delicious Neil.

NEIL: Yeah, they're good aren't they? There's two different types of mustard, it's homemade I think. Do you want some coffee?

MATT & WILL: Yes!

(NEIL serves them coffee from a flask.)

NEIL: *(Seeing MATT's bloody nose.)* What happened to you?

MATT: I got attacked by a raven.

WILL: He got attacked by a raven. It's been chaos here.

MATT: I ran into the door.

NEIL: *(Seeing the beaver mess.)* What happened there?

(WILL stands in front of it to hide it.)

NEIL: Don't try and hide it I've seen it now.

MATT: He put his foot through it.

NEIL: I leave you alone for five minutes and you trash the place. It's probably worth a lot of money that. It's art.

WILL: That's not art.

MATT: It's art if the artist says it is.

(WILL choosing to ignore this.)

WILL: OK. Schedule. We have this and then go yes? Have you got any sugar?

NEIL: No, sorry.

WILL: Fuck!

(MATT gets back in the tub.)

WILL: OK, schedule. We will eat these and then we can go right? *(Sees MATT.)* What are you doing Matthew!? We are going!

(MATT ignores him. The Northern Lights begin and the sky goes green. The light around the model house also goes green.)

NEIL: Oh look.

MATT: Oh yeah.

WILL: Oh great. Now the sky's gone green. This is all we bloody need. Schedule! It's OK to go now right? Can we drive in the dark?

MATT: It's not dark, it's green.

WILL: Can we drive in the green?

NEIL: Well yes, but I'd rather not in this atmosphere.

WILL: Come again? Sorry Neil, what we do not need at this precise moment is a relationship councillor. What we do need is a cab driver and that's you. You drive us back to Reykjavik and shut up.

MATT: Actually, I'd be fascinated to hear Neil's take on 'the atmosphere'. Neil?

WILL: Matthew, please. Come on, we are going.

(WILL goes inside to get dressed.)

WILL: Come on everyone. We're changing. It's the changing time. We're clearing up. Let's go.

NEIL: It's a pretty good one.

MATT: Yeah. Oh look, the swirls.

NEIL: Yeah.

WILL: So what, it's bloody green!

MATT: How long will this last for, Neil?

NEIL: I don't know. Should be a few hours at least.

MATT: A few hours? Great.

(WILL shoots NEIL a look and NEIL retreats into the kitchen.)

WILL: *(Imploring, softer.)* Come on, Matthew. I understand what you're doing, but this is not the right moment to do it. Look I'm sorry. That's what you want to hear, right? I'm sorry. Can we just talk about this when we are back in Reykjavik? Matthew, we broke in here.

(MATT clinks bottle as before. Back to best man speech.)

MATT: 'But joking aside, what can I say about Will? I could talk about his generosity…I could talk about his sense of humour, but what I'd like to talk about is his loyalty. This is a man of his word.'

WILL: Matthew, can we –

MATT: A promise is a promise, Will.

(Beat.)

(WILL marches off into the wilderness. NEIL enters.)

NEIL: Right, well I've cleared up a bit back there, there's just out here to do really. Has it stopped bleeding?

MATT: More or less.

NEIL: Friendship eh?

MATT: It's a bloody mess.

NEIL: A bit of chaos never did anyone any harm. You'll both come out the other end.

MATT: Is that what happened to you?

NEIL: God no, my life's a shit storm.

(Beat.)

NEIL: Where's Will?

MATT: I don't know.

NEIL: What do you mean you don't know?

MATT: He's gone off.

NEIL: Where? What, out there?

MATT: Yes. It's what he does.

NEIL: You bloody idiot, it's – 20 degrees out there, he'll die of exposure. You're not in bloody Clapham now.

MATT: I don't know.

NEIL: *(Shouting into the wilderness.)* Will!

MATT: I'm sorry Neil…

NEIL: Will!!! Right, call him. Just get out there and call him!!

(NEIL exits to bedroom, cursing.)

MATT: Will!

(WILL can be heard somewhere, shouting incoherently.)

MATT: Will! Just come back!

(WILL's shouts are fainter now.)

NEIL: *(From off.)* Can you hear him?

MATT: I can hear him. Will, I'm sorry! Alright? Just come back. Please.

(Nothing from WILL.)

NEIL: I thought you were supposed to be best mates.

MATT: Will? Will? I can't hear him.

(NEIL emerges in full bright orange rescue suit, holding flares.)

NEIL: Right, take these. They're flares.

MATT: Flares?

NEIL: Only use them in an emergency or the coast guard will send their helicopter out for us! Stay here, don't make too much noise and don't let anyone or anything in.

MATT: What would I – *(NEIL closes door.)*

(MATT mouths 'let in?')

WILDERNESS

(MATT stands alone.)

(Pause.)

(Noises under house begin – bangs. Then the RAVEN appears, flapping around his head, forcing him to seek sanctuary up the ladder. Quiet. Low rumbling begins, growing louder, the same noise as the tremor earlier but more intense. The stage now shakes and chairs bounce across the stage of their own accord until finally it fades. Quiet. Now the RAVEN returns and lands. MATT shoos it with the flares then waves them around his head and sets off stereo, which plays 'Isis' by Bob Dylan. This is the underscore for the whole scene in the wilderness.)

(MATT runs out of the house shouting to NEIL, then runs back in. More bangs under the house. MATT waves his arms to turn the music down. The music gets louder.)

(Cut to – WILL alone in wilderness in appalling weather. NEIL and MATT operate leaf blower and blow snow on WILL. WILL walks out of the image.)

(Cut to – NEIL in wilderness in pursuit of WILL, calling after him – WILL helps MATT create the image with the blower and snow. NEIL

walks out of the image.)

(Cut to – WILL, dropping to his knees in the snow and the wind. The model house is lit and blaring out 'Isis'. NEIL exits behind the screen.)

(Cut to – MATT is in the house still trying to turn off stereo. He jumps down off the sofa. The stereo stops. He sits down. The stereo comes back on again.)

(The landline phone rings and MATT answers. We hear the voice on the other end. It is a deep voice, speaking Icelandic. This is GUNNI, a Reykjavik gangster. The translation appears scrolling across the dot matrix screen.)

MATT: Hello?

GUNNI: Hello? Who is this? *(What we hear on the phone – 'Hver er Thetta?')*

MATT: Hello… Oh god… I don't speak Icelandic… I'm…my name is Matthew…

GUNNI: 'Are you with that mother fucker? We know he's there. Where is Neil?' *(Phone – 'Ertu med thessum helvítis fauvita? Vid vitum ad hann er tharna. Hvar er Neil?')*

MATT: Neil? Yes we have a Neil…Neil…he was here, but he's out there no…er… *(Picks up a laminate and reads.)* Help me. 'Eg var vithskila vid hopinn.' *(I've become separated from the group.)*

GUNNI: Group? What group? *(To someone else.)* Who the fuck is this prick? *(To MATT.)* Listen to me asshole. You tell Neil we're on our way. We know he's in one of those houses. We know he has the money. And we will make him pay. Slowly. *(Phone – Houp? Hvada houp? Hvaða fáviti er þetta? Hlustadu au mig fíflid thitt. Segdu Neila að við séum að koma. Við vitum að hann er í einu af þessum húsum. Vid vitum ad hann er med peningana. Og vid lautum hann borga. Haegt!!!!)*

(During this MATT is trying to interrupt saying, 'I don't understand. Emergency. They're out there'.)

(The line goes dead.)

MATT: Hello? Hello?

(The cow appears naked in just a towel heading for the hot tub. He stops when he sees MATT. Stand off. The cow backs off apologetically and disappears.)

(RAVEN flapping. RAVEN appears on top of the screen in his light. VO of the RAVEN talking in Bob Dylan's voice.)

RAVEN: 'Hey Matt. Have you ever seen a moth attack a light bulb?'

MATT: *(Nods.)* Yes.

RAVEN: 'It's because he thinks it's the moon'.

(RAVEN flies away, 'Isis' increases to very loud.)

MATT: No, wait!

(Cut to – WILL in wilderness. He is on the edge of the Kingsjongur Crevice. He takes a deep breath and dives.)

(MATT covers WILL with a dust sheet.)

NEIL: *(From O/S.)* Will, no!

(Seen through the sheet WILL looks like he's underwater. The music supports this as 'Isis' becomes muted and distorted. MATT slowly pulls the sheet over WILL and off him. WILL stands still. When the sheet is clear of him he is wet and holding a large rock. 'Isis' reverts to the loud volume of previously.)

(NEIL runs to WILL to help him out of the crevice. WILL, terrified and confronted by a monstrous figure looming over him in an orange jumpsuit with goggles, hits NEIL with the rock. MATT makes the noise of the hit on the DS microphone.)

THE OFFERING

(Cut to – MATT in the house, dancing to 'Isis'.)

(Light up on WILL struggling back to the house.)

(Back to MATT continuing to dance.)

(Light on both, they see each other. Beat.)

(MATT opens the door and WILL staggers in. WILL seems to be offering the rock to MATT. He drops the rock and the boom is amplified. 'Isis' stops. They watch the rock until it comes to rest. Quiet. WILL falls to the floor, exhausted. MATT attends to him and props him up.)

MATT: Sit up. Come on.

WILL: *(Shivering and half dead. Muttering feverishly.)* There's a horse.

MATT: *(Removing his drenched t-shirt.)* Let's get this off.

WILL: There's an orange giant.

MATT: Orange? That's Neil. You saw Neil?

WILL: Where's Neil? Who's Neil?

MATT: Neil! Neil! He's wearing a suit.

    (Pause.)

WILL: That seems excessively formal of him.

MATT: What happened to Neil?

WILL: I think I hit him.

MATT: You hit Neil? Did he go down?

WILL: He did go down.

MATT: Did he get up?

WILL: He did not get up.

    (A flare lights up the sky in the distance.)

MATT: That's him… I'll fire back.

    (He hurriedly reads the instructions and fires flare from the terrace.)

MATT: Or have I just told him *we're* in danger? I'll do another.

(Fires a second flare.)

(Still lying on the floor inside.)

WILL: It's not bloody texting.

MATT: I don't know. I'll send another.

WILL: No.

(They wrestle over the flare and it fires into the kitchen.)

WILL: It's gone in the kitchen.

MATT: Oh god.

(Cut to – NEIL in wilderness. He sees the two flares fire from the model house, a red LED-controlled above the model by MATT and WILL.)

NEIL: Oh for fuck's sake.

(Cut to – Back in the house. MATT and WILL are in the kitchen dealing with a fire.)

WILL: Get the fire extinguisher. Just pull the nozzle.

MATT: I'm reading, I'm reading –

(Sound of extinguisher going off. Smoke billows out from the kitchen and across the stage.)

WILL: Aaah!

MATT: I'm sorry, I'm sorry.

WILL: Give me it.

MATT: Wait.

(WILL emerges with the fire extinguisher.)

WILL: Get out of the way!

(He fires it back into the kitchen.)

MATT: Aaah!

WILL: Well if you stand in the way!

(The fire is now out.)

MATT: You are telling Neil about this.

WILL: It's not his house.

MATT: Well then you are writing a note.

WILL: You want me to write a note?

MATT: Yes.

WILL: 'Dear owner of the summer house. I am one of the three little pigs who kicked back in your house tonight. I am afraid we have a few apologies to make. Exclamation mark. Amongst other things, we damaged your kitchen with a flare and had a little accident with one of your objets d'art. Although there was some debate as to its artistic merits.'

(During this they have emerged from the kitchen. Their faces and torsos are white from the fire extinguisher.)

NEIL'S RETURN – SACRED LAND

(They see NEIL standing outside. He is in bad shape. WILL opens the door to let him in and NEIL goes to hit him. WILL moves and MATT gets hit on the nose.)

(WILL hits NEIL in return. NEIL hits WILL. They all collapse. MATT closes the door and tries to attend to WILL and NEIL.)

(Pause.)

(They are all utterly exhausted. WILL and NEIL start laughing.)

NEIL: *(Noticing and silently studying the rock.)* Is that it?

WILL: I did the dive!

NEIL: *(Still exhausted.)* You're supposed to throw it back in. If you take the rock out you throw it back in. Do you not understand? This is sacred shit.

MATT: It's just a rock, Neil.

NEIL: *(Surprisingly intense.)* Nothing is just a rock round here. Don't you understand? You'll wake the land up. You'll wake the gods up.

WILL: Fuck off.

NEIL: No. I live here I've seen this shit. You have to take it back.

MATT: What?

NEIL: You have to take it back!

WILL: *(Rising.)* OK, OK.

MATT: No, you stay I'll go. I can do this.

(MATT rises and starts to prepare.)

NEIL: There are repercussions when you take things that don't belong to you! You'll have volcanoes erupting, earthquakes ripping across the land. There'll be hordes of undead Viking warriors roaming around.

MATT: Where's my coat?

NEIL: *(Smiling and pushing his luck, inventing wildly.)* There'll be flying polar bears eating hot dogs and watching late night Icelandic quizzes.

WILL: *(Cottoning on.)* That's not funny.

MATT: *(Also realising.)* No. No.

(Laughing at them. Then serious.)

NEIL: *(To WILL.)* You, fucking nutter. *(To MATT.)* You, nutter.

NEIL: *(To WILL.)* You could have died down there.

WILL: Whoah. Everybody be cool.

(He throws an empty beer bottle, which smashes.)

(WILL laughs.)

NEIL: That's it. You guys are off the charts. I'm finding another stag party. I'm joining the Sheffield lot.

WILL: This is beyond Sheffield!

NEIL: *(Exiting behind the screen.)* If I'm ever on a operating table and I wake up to see one of you, I'll know I'm fucked.

WILL: You won't wake up on his operating table, because he's not a surgeon!

MATT: Oh OK. Now I'm bringing this!

(He jumps on WILL as if wrestling.)

WILL: Neil, help! Hit him with the rock!

NEIL: *(Emerges from kitchen.)* They found a bloody teenager down there!

WILL: What can I say; the teenager obviously didn't cut it.

NEIL: What happened to the kitchen?

(Beat.)

WILL: We had to destroy that kitchen. Rich foreigners get no sympathy from us, Neil.

(NEIL is still. Then he picks up a bottle and smashes it.)

NEIL: Fair enough.

(WILL cheers and rises.)

(WILL and NEIL proceed to smash bottles in turn.)

(MATT has picked up the rock and he smashes it through the sliding door/window with a scream.)

(At the point of impact, the action freezes. Lights and sound change. Slowly MATT, outside time, steps down to the terrace and places the rock on the ground. He calmly brings three pieces of glass and places them around the rock. He brings a large jagged piece of glass and slots it in the corner of the set – the remainder of the smashed window. MATT returns to the position he was in when he stopped.)

(The lights and sound snap back to how they were.)

(They react to the sudden smashed window. The wind is now present. MATT giggles and is breathing hard. He steps down onto the terrace.)

The others walk over to him, intrigued. MATT walks barefoot across the glass. Sound cue of crunching glass with each footfall.)

RITUALS

(TIMESHIFT – Lighting effect of the negative photograph as before, and swirling wind crescendo. The three walk into position during this, by the veranda. Lights and sound snap back and they jump into the action.)

(They take it in turns to navigate across the shards of broken glass on the terrace like a walking-on-hot-coals-corporate-bonding exercise; NEIL runs across barefoot, shrieking. WILL hops across on one barefoot. MATT drops to his knees and shuffles across. NEIL pulls down his pants and sits on the glass. They all cheer. Accompanying wind.)

(TIMESHIFT – as before.)

(They dance, variations on formal partner dancing, to 'When the Swallows Come Back to Capistrano' by The Ink Spots, which plays on the stereo.)

(TIMESHIFT.)

(NEIL is pouring the vodka down the necks of MATT and WILL who are sitting on the sofa. Giant footsteps getting nearer and louder. They look up. We hear THUNKATAR, his voice a long way away – 'There was a young woman named Ygdrasil…oh fuck it'. The footsteps move away, the three follow him with their eyes.)

(TIMESHIFT.)

(They dance and cut themselves with a piece of the glass, in turn. MATT cuts WILL. 'Is This Love' by Bob Marley blares out from the stereo.)

(A TIMESHIFT.)

(WILL and MATT are seated DS looking out over the audience towards THOR who is unseen. NEIL is hovering US near the ladder.)

WILL: *(Mid-conversation.)* You see, you're just taking too much on, Thor. I mean, you should try just talking to her.

THOR: *(Voice over.)* Maybe, maybe. Alright, well listen, just drop the rock back on your way back and we'll say no more about it.

WILL & MATT: Absolutely. Yes.

THOR: *(Voice over – from time to time we hear him wrestling with his cloak.)* What are all these houses doing here? This is sacred land! These will all have to go! Add it to the bloody list. I'd make yourself scarce if I were you.

WILL & MATT: Of course, no problem. Thanks, Thor.

NEIL: And lose the cloak…

THOR: *(Voice over.)* Really? Loki, is that you?

(NEIL looks away.)

THOR: Hmm. OK. *(Sound of him wrestling with the cloak and setting off – faintly.)* Lose the cloak. Interesting.

(TIMESHIFT.)

(WILL and NEIL are out in the wilderness, hunting for the lost beaver. MATT is standing in the house wearing NEIL's jacket. Wind.)

NEIL: Where is it?

WILL: Where did you flick it? Beaver?

NEIL: Beaver?

(We hear a phone ring.)

WILL: Matthew, I've found your phone! *(Answers it.)* Hello? Oh hi John. Yeah that was us yeah… Well, it's complicated but…

NEIL: Beaver!! I've found the beaver!

WILL: John? …John?

(MATT discovers two wads of money in NEIL's coat pockets. He holds them in front of him and looks at them.)

(A TIMESHIFT.)

(NEIL is offstage. WILL and MATT are sat with beaver in hand, dissecting it expertly. Classical music plays on the stereo.)

WILL: That's the pulmonary artery there. *(Beat. They are confused.)* Hold on, where's the heart?

(NEIL emerges from the kitchen, face now white like the others.)

(TIMESHIFT.)

(They are gathered around a hole in the terrace. A floorboard has been prised up. 'I Just Died in Your Arms Tonight' by The Cutting Crew plays from the stereo in the background.)

WILL: Oh little beaver. Or maybe you are a squirrel. We don't really know. You were released tonight from your strange home by three strange men. But all men are strange beaver. As I'm sure you would have been, if you had grown to be a man like us. If you are a male that is. And a beaver. And if we are men.

(Beaver is laid to rest – mimed.)

WILL: *(Holding the next beaver.)* Oh little beaver –

(TIMESHIFT.)

(The three stand, shouting to the gods – 'I have become separated from my group' in Icelandic. They throw the cash into the air and it floats down.)

'Vith Vithskila vith hopinn!!'

(There is a tremor. It is bigger than before. Everything moves around. They celebrate.)

(Viking waltz music and lighting cross-fade. They stay exactly where they are and cross their wrists in front of them as before as they form the Jomsviking queue.)

JOMSVIKING QUEUE 3

WILL: Tord! Tord!

(Pause.)

WILL: Oh sorry mate, you look like a friend of mine.

MATT: I'm up. See you up there.

WILL: Put the hair up mate.

MATT: Don't start.

(MATT, as Jomsviking, steps up to the scaffold to be beheaded.)

MATT: Right where do you want me? Is one of you sorry lot going to hold my hair back?

NEIL: It's famed across the land as a symbol of our tribe.

MATT: It's the least you could do. Oi you.

(WILL is now a terrified Norwegian.)

WILL: No sorry sir, sorry sir, no no.

MATT: Yes you. You lucky Norwegian prick come here. Gather it up. Go on. All of it! Wrap it round your wrists! Pull it! Tighter!

MATT: *(To NEIL, who is now the axe man.)* Oi, pretty boy, are you going to kill me or what?

(NEIL, as executioner, moves towards him and swings his axe.)

(MATT pulls his head away from the block, pulling WILL's hands onto it. They all freeze for a split second.)

(WILL then screams and runs away looking at his stumps. MATT laughs and toys with his hair.)

NEIL: *(As narrator.)* The king of Norway was so impressed with this act of trickery that he spared not only the life of this Joms warrior, but the remainder of the tribe.

(All three cheer and break their shackles.)

WILL: *(As Joms again.)* What did you do that for?

MATT: What?

WILL: I wanted to go to Valhalla, didn't I?

MATT: *(Thinking.)* Oh.

(They all sing to the tune of 'You Are My Sunshine' as they travel back to the tub and sit.)

ALL: 'We are Joms Vikings, super Joms Vikings'
We go a-raping when skies are grey
We hate you Sweden, we hate you Denmark,
But most of all we hate you bastard Norway'
Joms Joms, Norway scums.

HOT TUB 3 – SO WHERE'S THE NEXT BATTLE BOYS?

(Pause. The three are seated in the hot tub. It is windy and they are all cold.)

WILL: So where's the next battle then boys?

(Pause. Distant sound of a helicopter flying past. They watch it impassively until it disappears again.)

MATT: I've got the boiler man coming on Tuesday.

NEIL: Is it a 'Combi?'

MATT: Yeah.

NEIL: They phased the old ones out here. They are all combis.

WILL: Matt, have you got the disposable cameras for the tables?

MATT: Will, 'I'll see what I can do.'

(They smile.)

(Pause.)

WILL: So Neil, this money… How much trouble are you in?

(NEIL looks around at the money scattered everywhere, almost surprised by it.)

NEIL: Well…

(Pause.)

(The phone rings.)

MATT: Oh, your friend phoned earlier. Icelandic chap. Deep voice.

(NEIL gets up and goes to the phone. He answers.)

NEIL: Hallo Gunni.

GUNNI: Hallo Neil *(On dot matrix screen – 'Hello Neil').*

NEIL: Svo thou fannst mig.

GUNNI: Vid erum alveg ad koma. Thu getur flúith ef thu vilt gera thetta enn skemmtilegra. *(We're almost there. You can run away if you want to make it more fun?')*

NEIL: Nei, ég fer ekki rassgat. Eg verd herna!!!

GUNNI: Eg held ad thu aettir ad segja hinum ad fara, er thad ekki? *(I think you'd better tell your friends to go don't you?'.)*

NEIL: Ju, eg geri thad.

WILL: Is it a Worcester?

MATT: No, it's a Vaillant.

GUNNI: Thu tokst peningana okkar Neil. Madur bara gerir ekki soleidis. Ha!? Thath hefur sinar afleidingar thegar madur tekur hluti sem madur au ekki. *(You took our money Neil. You shouldn't have done that eh? There are repercussions when you take things that don't belong to you.)*

NEIL: Eg veit. Fyrirgefdu madur.

(NEIL hangs up.)

WILL: Worcester's the best.

MATT: I think they are much of a muchness.

WILL: I've talked to a plumber and he said they put a fault in them so they clap out after six years.

MATT: I've got an eight year guarantee. Eight years.

(NEIL returns.)

NEIL: You'll never get eight years out of it.

(Pause. NEIL holds out car key.)

NEIL: You better go.

MATT: *(Disappointed.)* Oh.

WILL: Why, is someone coming?

NEIL: Yeah.

WILL: Are they coming here? Now?

NEIL: That's what he said.

MATT: Neil, just say the word and we will bring it.

(They look at MATT and he realises they need to go. He takes the car key.)

WILL: What are you going to do, Neil?

NEIL: Something'll turn up.

(He sits back in the tub. Quiet faraway rumble – a gathering storm. The rumble gets louder and nearer. The house begins to shake and the lights flicker. The noise builds to a deafening crescendo until the house finally breaks apart in an earthquake – the staging has split apart, steam pours out through the gaps. Then silence.)

NEIL: That should keep them busy for a while.

LOKI'S CHAOS SONG

(The Viking waltz begins again.)

WILL: Who are you, Neil?

(NEIL begins to talking in verse.)

NEIL: I'm just a fall guy for the big man.
It's chaos but I put a good show on.
I drift around town, I'm up and I'm down.
(Singing now.) And so on, and so on, and so on.

(MATT passes a guitar to NEIL from under the stage. NEIL plays along to the waltz.)

(Full singing now, out to the audience.)

I was there at the treaty of Versailles.

(MATT & WILL – 'Versailles, Versailles'.)

I was there at the sacking of Rome.

(MATT & WILL – 'Rooaaame'.)

I'm there when you cry, when you kiss your wife goodbye
(All.) And so on, and so on, and so on.
(MATT clinks bottles in time with the music.)
I blew the iceberg in front of Titanic
I played cards with Marlon Brando
I drove Diana's car pissed, but I wrote Schindler's list,
And I will just go on and go on.

Oh it's so hard to be me

(MATT & WILL 'Poor him'.)

(MATT and WILL rise. Then dance and twirl on to the house.)

Hotels and whiskey and late night TV
I asked head office if I could be free
They said it's all there in clause 14c
(All.) You're ours, you'll never be free
It goes on and on and on.

(Instrumental – The house starts thumping its own waltz rhythm in time with the music.)

(WILL, produces and plays harmonica.)

(MATT goes behind screen. He reappears as the cow in just the towel as before, still waiting to use the hot tub. Cow goes back behind the screen shaking his head.)

(MATT puts up RAVEN behind the screen in its light before coming back out.)

(MATT and WILL gather up their clothes in preparation to leave.)

(NEIL puts the guitar down and remains sitting in the tub.)

(ALL LOUDLY FOR FINAL VERSE.)

He's just an unemployed conman
Come on be fair, you all know one
He puts on his best face, for every new place
And so on and so on and so on

(MATT and WILL look to NEIL, then each other, then exit.)

NEIL: *(Alone.)* And so on, and so on, and so on

(NEIL looks up at the RAVEN. He goes over to model house and stands over it. Lights go down on the rest of the set leaving only the model and the RAVEN illuminated. He takes the model car and sets it off on a journey across the stage. He lights it with the torch as the other lights, and the music, fade. He switches off the torch.)

(Blackout.)

The End.

WWW.OBERONBOOKS.COM

Follow us on www.twitter.com/@oberonbooks
& www.facebook.com/oberonbook